The Guide to

HONEST

PARENTING

Daniel Craven

This book is dedicated to...

My parents, Paul and Kathryn Craven, without whom I would not have had the education and life experience that I've been fortunate to have.

My Grand mother, Grandfather, and Me-mom, whose wisdom gave me a glimpse into what our world was like early in the 20th Century.

My brother, Brad Craven, for teaching me what it's like to have a sibling, after being an only child for 9 years...whether he meant to, or not.

Aunt Mary Ann and Uncle Tom for putting me in my place when I needed it.

Roy Hamley, Ed.D for all that you taught me about Psychology, and for being a good person and a friend to all.

Philip, Jackson and Evan, for giving me a different perspective on parenting.

Parents and children throughout the world. The most important thing to us should be LIFE and the preservation of it. The second most important thing should be the quality of it.

CONTENTS:

CONGRATULATIONS! By purchasing The Guide to Honest Parenting, you've shown that you CARE about your relationship with your child or teen. And… that you care about improving your child's or teen's behavior and relieving your "parental stress!" Being a frustrated or overwhelmed parent, as many of you are, it may be difficult to find the energy and even… the love… to keep trying. Well, you've made a good decision and I am proud of you for that! I bring this information to you as a friend, because I want it to be a positive, comfortable transition for you to move from things that haven't been working, to things that will work. Also, I do offer support…not just a book that leaves you hanging. It doesn't matter where you are on the 1-10 scale of parenting. What matters is that you are at a point where you are willing to learn and try a new way.

This information is not bound by race, religion, gender, political beliefs, sexual orientation, or national origin. While some cultural beliefs may affect how you are used to children being raised, you wouldn't be reading this if what you have already tried was working. The world is a different place than it was in 1950 or 1960, or 1970, or even 1980. So, the way that we respond to kids must adapt… although this parenting style would have worked from the beginning of my grandparents' generation. This is designed for use with children and teens from age 2 and up, but can even be effective with adults. I truly believe that if all of the kids in the world were raised with love, and using the information contained in this book, our prisons would not be overcrowded, and we could still leave our houses and cars unlocked, without fear. That would have a dramatic effect on our freedom and safety. It would also improve the economy, because we could save billions of dollars that are spent housing inmates and building and maintaining prisons.

I know that it's not always easy raising children. Well, actually… it's RARELY easy. Being a parent can be a tremendous challenge! However, it can also be a tremendously rewarding experience! I want you to have as many positive, FUN moments with your child or teen as you can possibly have the opportunity to enjoy. For some of you, FUN may seem like something that can't happen. PLEASE don't be discouraged!

Deciding which parenting style or "program" to use in relating to your child and dealing with behavioral or emotional issues is a big deal, because you have to have open-mindedness about the method, and you have to invest your time, energy, and love in using that method with someone whom you care about. There are MANY books and "programs" out there. Some work better than others, and some don't work at all. Some are advertised heavily… and that certainly doesn't mean that they are better. I've reviewed MANY parenting books and several "programs," and while I didn't find one that I would entirely agree with, I do know that this one can give you the progress that you're looking for, if you are dedicated to it.

Some of you are parents by careful planning. Others became parents by accident, or by entering into a relationship with someone who already had children. Some of you are part of a growing group of GRANDparents who are raising their childrens' children. In any case, I'm glad that you're here.

I realize that what most of us know about parenting comes from our own parents and how they raised us. Sometimes that's OK, and sometimes, we need more information… or completely different information. It's been said at least a thousand times… "Kids don't come with instruction books." If I only had a dime for every time I heard THAT one! But… it's true. And, while you might think that there are no more "new ideas" or "breakthroughs" in parenting… sometimes, an open mind can be your best parenting skill. Also, even ideas that have been used before can be refined.

Why "HONEST PARENTING"? I use the term "HONEST" because what I am presenting is a way of relating to children and adolescents that is free of "reverse psychology," power struggles, manipulation, outsmarting them, yelling, punishing, spanking, or otherwise belittling them… or using other tactics that tear relationships apart. This information is based on creating a POSITIVE relationship, in which the parent is in control of the home, but the CHILD or ADOLESCENT is more in control of their own choices and decisions… because they become ABLE and WILLING to make GOOD choices and decisions. It is much easier to parent a child who consistently makes GOOD choices, than to spend your time and energy MAKING the child do things that you expect him / her to do.

2

This information is based on the idea that a child or adolescent, no matter how "bad" their behavior…is a person worth building a relationship with. It is based on the idea that they have VALUE as human beings. And… it is based on the idea that they are intelligent enough to communicate with, to teach, and to build relationships with. What your child or teen needs from

YOU is love, patience, an open mind, and the ENERGY to use what you are about to read, consistently and to the best of your ability. No one is perfect. When it comes to you AND your child or teen, we are shooting for 100% effort, while knowing that sometimes, 80% is good enough for a night when everyone is tired.

By the time most parents find Honest Parenting, they are already tired, frustrated, and have tried things like counseling, Psychiatrists (medications), and possibly hospitalization or residential care. No book or "program" can possibly answer EVERY question that you have, and no book or "program" can know your exact situation and the specific things that you and your child or teen say to each other and how your child or teen responds to you. That's why I offer email and phone coaching, as well as to answer your questions in the email newsletter. Please sign up for the newsletter by sending an email to: support@honestparenting.com.

I want EVERY family who uses Honest Parenting to be successful and some of you will need support to make that happen. **Whether you seek coaching from me, are involved with a counselor or therapist in your area, or whether you use this parenting style alone, I ask that you stay focused on Honest Parenting, and that you do not become distracted by other information or other parenting styles. It's just more successful and less confusing if you are working with one approach, than if you are working with someone who teaches something different.** There are many GREAT mental health professionals out there…I just want to be sure that you can focus on ONE method that I KNOW can help!

OK… just one expectation. NO SMOKING CRACK as you read this! Smoking crack while learning parenting skills may cause the information to become distorted.

Here's the serious part... This information that you're reading is just that... information. In bringing this to you, I am not offering "therapy," "treatment," or "advice." Not knowing you or your family's specific situation, and not being with you to see how you use this information, I cannot guarantee any certain level of results or improvement. I will try to explain the techniques and ideas in terms that are easy to understand, and will also use examples.

If your child or adolescent is physically harmful to himself / herself, or others, I encourage you to get local help. The information still applies to hurtful, physically aggressive children and adolescents...in fact it applies just as much, if not MORE, to kids who are out of control. However, SAFETY comes first, and progress is a process. I don't want anyone to be in physical danger while learning this information and trying to make the level of progress needed to get past a child's violence.

There are certain ways that a child may be held, therapeutically, for his / her safety and for the safety of others, but I do not recommend or teach these, because I cannot be with you to teach them effectively, or to help you decide when they are appropriate to use. Please leave therapeutic holding to professionals and feel free to contact me if you would like an opinion about whether the method of a program that you are using is appropriate or effective.

As a therapist, I have been hit, kicked, bitten, pinched, spit on, and attempted to be injured with everything from rocks to knives to the point of a drawing compass. I have even had a gun pulled on me. I do not want you to be in these situations. So... if your child has these behaviors, get local help first. THEN...PLEASE read this book... because you need to resolve these issues in a SUCCESSFUL way, and you need to do it before your child gets bigger, stronger, and in serious trouble in the community. If your child is small, or if their hurtfulness is mild and tolerable for you, then you can make your own decision regarding outside help. However, physical safety comes first!

You get one shot at shaping your child's life and causing them to be independent, productive adults. Fortunately, it's at least an 18-year shot! However, if you think that being a parent is expensive, think about how expensive it would be if your child was 30 years old and was still financially dependent on you! Let's do it RIGHT, so that they can take care of YOU when you're old!

Now that you've put down your crack pipe, let's get started, shall we?

Where should we start? At the BEGINNING, of course! Now, I understand that it's tempting to skip to a chapter that is the "meat" of the answer that you're looking for. How many times have we all bought something and not read all of the instructions? OK… do that, if you like…but I STRONGLY encourage you to read this information in its entirety at some point, because understanding how your child's behavior and your relationship got to their current states… AND… understanding how a child's emotional and behavioral development occurs… will help you to make progress.

Throughout this book, you will see some phrases and ideas repeated. This is done because they are important, and because we learn by repetition.

As you are reading, please keep in mind that the way that I view a child or adolescent with behavioral or emotional issues is this…

The child or teen, for whatever reason, is not using behaviors that are appropriate for his or her age. The child or teen is experiencing a delay in his or her emotional development, which also affects social interactions, coping and problem-solving skills, and having appropriate and fulfilling relationships with family members. His or her interactions with people in the community are also affected. His or her behavior can sometimes be annoying, disgusting, or disappointing, but may also be dangerous or criminal in some cases. He or she is also a human being, has some good traits, and can develop into a wonderful, amazing person… with help. He or she may have mild, moderate, or severe issues, but the information in this book applies to all of these.

See your child or teen as being 2-3 years old inside, but having an older body. A popular term for this condition is "arrested development." Let's see if we can eliminate "arrests" from your family, altogether.

NOTES:

CHAPTER 1

TRUST IS THE FOUNDATION OF ANY RELATIONSHIP.

Let me say that again...

TRUST IS THE FOUNDATION OF ANY RELATIONSHIP.

You trust your postal carrier not to read your mail...even though you may not know them. You trust your hair stylist to give you a nice haircut. You trust your co-workers not to steal from your purse or desk. These aren't even your closest relationships. Trusting your CHILD is SUPER-IMPORTANT to you being able to feel comfortable allowing them to have less supervision. It's also important you YOUR stress level, because if you can't trust them, then you do a LOT of work keeping an eye on them and worrying. Your child or teen being able to trust YOU is the FIRST step in building a positive relationship. A parent must show a child or teen that they love them, that they are safe to be around, and that they are honest and in control of themselves. I want to help you to be a confident parent...one who knows how to handle any situation. Then, your child or teen will respect you and trust you to be in charge.

HOW DID MY KID GET TO BE THIS WAY??

Before we see progress in a child's or adolescent's behavior, we have to look at what causes them to use poor choices and behaviors. There are several possibilities for why your child is not making appropriate decisions and for why your relationship is in its current place. We need to look at your child's TRUST LEVEL and ENVIRONMENT, in order to understand things that may have caused problems... to possibly recognize things that you, as a parent, may be able to do in order to give the child the best starting position… and to give yourself the easiest road to travel toward the top of the mountain.

WHAT IS TRUST?

As of February, 2009, the Merriam-Webster online dictionary defines trust and trustworthiness in the following ways…

TRUST: assured reliance on the character, ability, strength, or truth of someone or something

2: one in which confidence is placed

3: dependence on something future or contingent

TRUSTWORTHINESS: a charge or duty imposed in faith or confidence or as a condition of some relationship

OK… so, in plain language, as it applies to you and your child…

TRUST (For your Child or Teen): Your child needs to be able to rely on your character, your ability to care for him / her, and your strength as a person and as a parent. Your child needs to be able to place confidence in you to be there, to love, teach, and provide food, water, shelter, medical care, a safe, sanitary and physically healthy environment, an environment that is also emotionally healthy, and to give him / her positive attention and nurturing. Your child needs to know that you will set limits and boundaries for him or her, and that you will do this with the heart and mindset of a teacher or mentor, or... of a loving parent. Your child needs to have faith that in the future, you will continue to respond in a consistent way to him / her... that you will react in the same ways that you usually do, when similar incidents occur. This does NOT mean that you can't change and improve upon the way that you react to your child... just that you are consistent in what you do and say, when you begin to use these techniques. You need to be somewhat predictable.

TRUST (For a Parent): You need to know that your child will make safe, responsible choices, even when you're not watching them... and knowing that they feel comfortable being honest with you and taking responsibility for their mistakes. To make them feel safe in taking responsibility for their mistakes, they need to know that you will not yell at them, punish them, or hurt them when they confess. Don't worry... if you use any of these responses, I have a replacement response for you, just as you will help your child or teen to replace THEIR inappropriate or non-working behaviors.

How do I get TRUST?

OK...first of all, I KNOW that some of you will be thinking... "WHY SHOULD I BUILD TRUST WITH MY CHILD? HE / SHE IS THE ONE WHO NEEDS TO BUILD TRUST WITH _ME!_ IT'S MY CHILD WHO IS DOING ALL OF THESE INAPPROPRIATE THINGS! IT IS MY CHILD WHO NEED TO START BEING TRUSTWORTHY!"

TRUST is "The Foot of the Mountain." It's the foundation of all relationships... the base that supports all other pieces of a relationship. Or, as in the diagram in this chapter, it's the center of the relationship, with communication, willingness to comply with your requests, and ability to have a mutually-satisfying relationship as possible benefits. Trust is also the first step in a child feeling safe in the world, and with you as a parent. I'm sorry that you can't buy TRUST at Wal-Mart or Target. But, if you could, it would be the most expensive item in the store, and would never go on sale…it's THAT valuable! OK…it's even more valuable than THAT!

Even though it may seem as though your child is the one who has the work to do, the parent is the LEADER in this journey. Your child or adolescent ALSO has work to do, but it is YOU who is raising THEM. And so… the PARENT models trustworthiness through being nurturing, firm, consistent, and in control of his / her own emotions. No one is perfect, we're just looking for "consistent."

TRUST and RESPECT are EARNED… in BOTH directions. The ideas that someone should respect me "because I'm an adult," or "because I'm the parent," are laughable. The achievements of living to a certain age or being biologically able to produce a baby are not reasons that we should be respected. We should be trusted and respected because of the way that we treat people and because of the good, honest choices that we make. Can you think of an adult that you don't respect? Our prisons are FULL of them (along with some innocent people, too… but that's another book). When the phrase "respect your elders" was put into use, I'm SURE that it meant "respect your elders… when they are worthy of respect."

Please keep in mind that you are there to guide, nurture, and teach your child… not to be responsible for their choices or behaviors. One goal is to help THEM to take responsibility for their choices… good or bad. That's how they gain the experience to be able to make good decisions as adults. If you are controlling, if you cater to them, or if you "smother" them, then they will remain dependent on you. This may meet some need of yours, or make you feel good while they are little… but be careful what you wish for! An "ADULT CHILD" who is financially or emotionally dependent on his / her parent is UN-FUN!

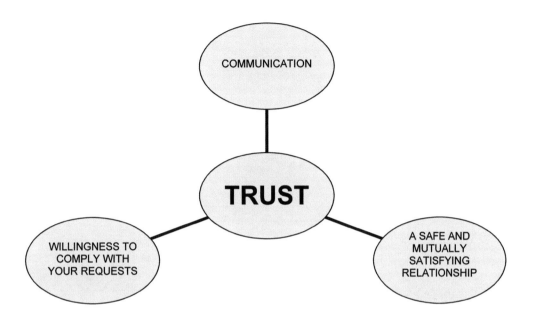

From the moment that your child was born, he or she began to develop a TRUST LEVEL. Do you trust EVERYONE the same amount? Of course not. Neither does a baby. That's one reason that a baby may cry when a certain person holds him or her... and be perfectly relaxed in the arms of someone like a mother or grandmother. So... if a baby doesn't really KNOW people, can't speak to them, and doesn't understand what they are saying, then how does the baby decide who to trust and who not to trust? It's based on senses.

Who holds me gently? Who feeds me? Who comes when I cry? Who smells familiar? Whose voice is pleasant and familiar? Who talks to me? Who changes my diaper? Who gives me positive attention? WHO LOVES ME?

Or... What face have I never seen before? What face looks mean? What voice is loud? Who handles me too roughly? Who pinches my cheeks? Who steals my pacifier?

EXAMPLE:

As a baby becomes a toddler, they can speak more and more words, and are more aware of what they expect from people around them. SAFETY is a BIG DEAL! When a child feels SAFE, he or she can begin to trust. What happens when a child wanders down an isle in a store for the first time and loses sight of mom or dad? They PANIC! They don't feel SAFE anymore. As they grow older, they become more comfortable going to the toy department by themselves. Of course...there are some children who wander off and talk to anyone. This is both good... and NOT so good. This behavior can be caused by a child being given an abundance of attention by many family members and friends, and visiting many different houses... so that they know MANY people at an early age and feel safe with all of them. Therefore, the child feels as though "EVERYONE IS OK TO BE AROUND."

Surely, you can see the danger in that. However, it can also mean that the child is extroverted, will make friends easily, and will be able to develop trusting relationships. Of course, you want to teach them NOT to wander off... and not by showing YOUR anxiety. THEY need to feel the anxiety in order to make good choices on their own (which, of course, is the ultimate goal). So... when you see them begin to wander off, keep them within eyesight, but hide around the end of the isle, where they can't see you. Then, when they don't see you, they will become anxious and scared, and will come looking for you. I don't suggest that you do this to be "mean," but only when, and if, they decide to leave your side. It will be a wonderful consequence for them to experience, because it will cause them to be aware of where you are... even when looking at toys. And... it will keep them from being easy prey for pedophiles, or from walking out into a busy street.

Trust is built on the consistency and predictability of the person.

If a child knows what you say to them in certain situations, when you will feed them, when it's time to go to school, when bedtime is, and how you respond to them when they make mistakes... then they are less anxious and more trusting. Inconsistency in a PARENT'S behavior causes a child to be confused, scared, anxious, and to be unable to relax and trust. Having a daily **ROUTINE** is also a big part of trust. Meal time, homework time and bed time should basically be the same times, each day. Of course, for parents with a work schedule that changes each week, or for kids in sports and other activities, adjustments need to be made. But... consistency is not rigidity.

A child or teen needs to know, feel, and BELIEVE that the parent will never tell them to do anything that is unsafe or against their best interest.

6 THINGS THAT DESTROY TRUST...

1. **Lack of nurturing, care, and affection, as an infant**

2. **Inconsistency in the caretaker's mood (severe mood swings)**

3. **Not being able to expect the same reactions from the caretaker when similar situations occur**

4. **A caretaker not setting clear limits or enforcing them**

5. **Physical or emotional neglect**

6. **Abuse... Physical, emotional, sexual, verbal, ritualistic**

 HOT TIP!

Abuse may be caused by a parent, relative, family acquaintance, someone at a daycare or school, babysitter, or stranger. Children have difficulty trusting people when they have been abused, and that means difficulty trusting ALL people... not just the abuser. Teens can be abused, also.

Abused kids are NOT "damaged goods"! Trust CAN be built with them! But... you have to practice HONEST PARENTING, and by this, I mean that **sincerity** is of the utmost importance.

If you are raising a child or teen in a home where abuse is NOW occurring by another family member… GET LOCAL HELP! If you are afraid of the abuser, or afraid to lose your child, then it's even MORE important to seek help. Children are DESTROYED by abuse, and their lives are basically over until it stops. Some suggestions would be to seek counseling, call your Department of Children's Services, have the abusive person leave, or leave with the victim. **If you allow abuse to occur, you will not be able to build trust or make progress with the child, and the child will have trouble trusting YOU, because they will not feel as though you can (or want) to protect them.**

Children who have difficulty trusting sometimes become **LEGALISTIC**. This means that they listen carefully to EVERY word that you say, and will hold you to any promises or statements that you make. **With children like this, it is VERY important not to tell them that you will do even the smallest thing, if you aren't 100% sure that you can follow through. Instead, use phrases like…**

 "We'll TRY to go to the park this afternoon."

"I MAY be able to take you to a movie this weekend."

Don't say "I'll take you to the park in a minute." Why? Because a legalistic child will time you on that minute using his or her watch or clock, and will call you on "lying" if you don't leave precisely when the minute is up.

Eventually, after you earn trust with the child, the legalism will decrease. Legalism is about not trusting people and holding them to every word that they say, because of some mistrust that has occurred in the past… not necessarily on your part, but in the child's life. Abandonment… someone not keeping promises… something where the child felt lied to or betrayed.

Have you ever been AFRAID to tell the truth?

If you have, then... WHY? You know that telling the truth is the right thing to do. What would make you, or your child... AFRAID to tell the truth? Could it be the REACTION that you might get from the person that you're talking to?

 TIP!

Make sure that your child or adolescent completely understands that you are not making a **promise**. Ask them to repeat what you've said **in their own words**. Make sure that they don't just repeat **your** words, because that doesn't require them to process the information. **Once they take responsibility for understanding... there is no room for confusion.**

EXAMPLE:

You find that the cookie jar is only half full, when you just filled it yesterday. Or... you find some money missing from the tray on your dresser. Whatever the case may be, you decide to confront your child about it. And... they deny it, completely.

Why wouldn't they just tell you the truth? Consider how you would react to them if they told the truth. AND... consider how any other caretakers that are present in the home would react. Would you (or another caretaker) yell at them? Be critical of them? Spank them? PUNISH them? These things are all scary to a child. I have a completely HONEST, PRODUCTIVE, and COMMON SENSE way of dealing with incidents where a child does something wrong or makes a mistake that will allow a child to feel comfortable telling you the truth and will ALSO cause them to become more mature and less likely to keep doing the same things. A child needs to feel SAFE in telling you that he / she has done something wrong or made a mistake. If a child doesn't trust that you are a safe person to tell the truth to, he / she will not feel comfortable talking freely.

How do I check my child's TRUST LEVEL?

Here's your "**TRUST-O-METER**." Ask yourself these questions...

- Can I leave my child or adolescent alone in his or her room for 10 minutes without worrying that he or she will hurt himself / herself or will destroy something? How about 20 minutes? 30 minutes?

- Does my child or adolescent shrink away from me, push me away, or leave the room when I try to hug him or her? Adolescents often go through a normal stage of not accepting physical affection from parents...but it's based on the idea that they are forming their own identity and that they look more to friends for approval. In other words, "parents aren't COOL." And..."It's embarrassing to be hugged by MOM or DAD." I know that this can be hurtful and disappointing to parents. It can be corrected, and can actually be a sign that your relationship needs improvement... but a certain amount of this is to be expected... especially in public or in the presence of others.

- Is my child or adolescent able to think of others and to do things for them because he or she values the relationship? Or... does he or she only do things for others when he or she WANTS SOMETHING?

- Is my child or adolescent SINCERE with other people, or does he or she have a "phony," "superficial" tone of voice?

- Does my child or adolescent use drama and act like he or she is in a Broadway play when I try to talk with him or her about something serious? Are his or her reactions overstated or meant to avoid talking? Avoidance is a sign of mistrust and testing limits.

- Does my child or adolescent lie? Cheat at games? Steal? Does he or she show REMORSE when he or she does something wrong or hurts someone's feelings?

- Does my child or adolescent hurt animals? People?

Honestly answering these questions should help you to determine whether or not your child has trust issues. If you find that your child DOES have trust issues, then CONGRATULATIONS! You've found your place to start!

 TIP!

The chapter on "COMMUNICATION" is VERY important in helping to build trust. A GREAT DEAL of your ability to build a trusting relationship with your child will be determined by how you communicate with him / her. A child will not communicate with you unless he / she TRUSTS you. A child will also not TRUST you, unless you communicate EFFECTIVELY with him / her. PLEASE pay careful attention to this chapter.

CHAPTER 2

ENVIRONMENT IS EVERYTHING!

CONGRATULATIONS on reading CHAPTER 1!
WELCOME to CHAPTER 2!

How's your environment today? Well, environments change, so it's important to think of the environments that your child has been in since birth. Of course, we know that children learn a large portion of what they know within the first 5 years of their lives. They are like "sponges." They absorb EVERYTHING that they see, smell, hear, touch, and taste. They develop their opinions of how safe their world is. They decide who is safe to be around. They learn to walk, talk, and hopefully, to count, spell... and possibly to read and write, operate a computer, and if we aren't careful... take over the WORLD!

How safe a child feels, how anxious or relaxed they are, and therefore, how well they learn, adapt, and mature emotionally has everything to do with their surroundings. I don't mean whether or not they live in a mansion and go to a private school. I mean that they need a safe home in order to be comfortable enough to grow emotionally and to mature appropriately. Ask yourself the following questions about your child's past AND present environments...

1. Have there been abusive people in the home?

2. Has my child been abused physically? Verbally? Emotionally? Sexually? Ritualistically?

3. Is my neighborhood safe?

4. Has my child always had a bed?

5. Has my child always had enough food?

6. Has my child had multiple caretakers and / or lived with different relatives or non-family members?

7. Has my child had a caretaker who is or was addicted to drugs / alcohol?

8. Has my child had a regular mealtime and bedtime routine?

9. Has my child lived in a home that was infested with insects or rodents?

10. Has my child lived in a home where he /she was traumatized? (Examples: Witnessed Robbery, Rape or any form of Violence?)

11. Has my child been excessively picked on by siblings or cousins?

12. Has my child lived in a home that was unusually dirty, messy or chaotic?

13. Has my child lived in a home where the water or electricity was often disconnected?

14. Has my child been homeless, or in a shelter?

I know that not all of these things will apply to everyone. And, if you answered "YES" to any of these, it does NOT mean that you aren't a good parent. In fact, no matter what has happened in the past… reading this book SHOWS that you are trying to be a GREAT parent! It's important to look at the home environment through the eyes of your child, to understand why he / she might have difficulty trusting, why he / she might not have developed emotionally to the age-appropriate level where he / she should be, and to discover any possible environmental barriers to your

relationship and to their development. If your child or teen treats you as an "EQUAL"… as a "PEER," then please understand that
it's because the child or teen does not feel safe or that you are in control. Your child or teen has either been allowed to develop a peer relationship with you because of your own need to have them as a "friend," or has decided that you are not demonstrating the confidence and ability to be the "PARENT."   If this is your situation, don't worry. You can change that!

Some of the circumstances listed above cannot be easily changed… and some (such as abuse), MUST be changed. I encourage you to eliminate any of those situations that are present in your home. Doing so will reduce your stress and will cause your child to feel more calm, safe, and OK with you being in charge.

If you have an abusive person in your home, I encourage you to make arrangements to leave or to have them leave, either by free will or with police. Please understand that you cannot usually force someone to leave a home that they own or pay rent for, or even a home that they have been residing in (without legal eviction procedures). So, plan carefully, but DO NOT live with an abusive person! It's unhealthy for you and your child. Your child's emotional development, behavior, and relationship with you cannot improve in that situation. Contact shelters, churches, your Department of Human Resources, or Police, at your own discretion.

If you are in poverty, then I suggest contacting a food bank, your Department of Human Resources, a church, relatives, the Red Cross, The Salvation Army, GoodWill, your city government branch that helps with utility bills, and any other community resources that you have.

TIP!

If any of the characteristics in the list, above, apply to your home NOW, please sign up for my newsletter by emailing us at support@honestparenting.com. I will do my best to help you improve your situation on an individual basis.

NOTES:

You're doing GREAT! You made it to CHAPTER 3, and you're still alive!!!!

HOW DO I GET MY CHILD TO "LISTEN"?

- Does your child or adolescent ignore you?

- Does your child or adolescent avoid sitting and talking with you?

- Does your child or adolescent often want to leave the dinner table?

- Do teachers or other professionals, or friends say that your child may have ADD or ADHD?

- Does your child use headphones while talking to you, roll their eyes, or face another direction, rather than looking at you?

- When you have a conversation, would your child or teen have trouble giving you a summary of what you talked about 10 minutes afterward?

I'll address ADD and ADHD, ODD, Conduct Disorder, etc. at the end of this chapter. There are also many other diagnoses that a child or teen can have, which Honest Parenting can be just as effective with. In fact, I would love it if you could just forget about any diagnoses that your child or teen may have and simply focus on the basics of this book. Sometimes, diagnoses make things more complicated than they have to be. We're working with a living, breathing, feeling PERSON… not a label or a list of symptoms.

First, we need to examine what it takes to get a child's or adolescent's attention. You need their attention in order to communicate with them, and in order to resolve problems as they arise.

What does it mean for your child to "LISTEN"?

Most parents associate the word "LISTEN" with doing whatever it is that you ask. However, a child may not understand that, and we need to be more specific with them. Let's try these…

"Could you please share the Play-Doh with your sister? It's the nice thing to do. Do you remember when I asked you to do that a few minutes ago? I really need for you to SHOW me that you can share the Play-Doh with her right now. Can you do that for me? Thanks! GREAT JOB! Now, can you please have fun

**without getting the Play-Doh in your sister's hair? Can you make me a car?
Can you make me a dog? What would you like to make with the Play-Doh?"**

See how specific that is? **Using words that make sense and give a child a NEW
behavior that is OK to use will help you to save time and frustration.**

Asking the child to make specific things with the Play-Doh, or even to choose
something that he or she wants to make, can **redirect** him or her from the conflict
and move the focus to something positive. Ahhhh… the power of a gentle
suggestion! Also, when I use examples with a child and you have a teenager (or
vice versa), please know that the same ideas apply to your child or teen, as well. I
try to use examples involving kids of all ages, but we're dealing with emotional
delays, so a teen who has a tantrum is really 3-years-old INSIDE, and if you have a
7-year-old, he or she will be a teen someday (so save those teen examples for
later). If a person uses 3-year-old behaviors, then EMOTIONALLY, they ARE 3-
years-old! Try to think of a situation in YOUR family where this example can be
applied.

STEP 1: CHECK YOURSELF BEFORE YOU WRECK YOURSELF!

Have you ever felt BETTER after losing your cool with your child? Have you ever
felt MORE SUCCESSFUL at solving a problem after yelling? The first step to
getting a child's attention is to be sure that you have a calm voice, relaxed posture,
and that you can state your expectations using kind words. Use words that express
HOW YOU FEEL… not hurtful or accusatory words. In doing this, you will be
TEACHING your child to do the same thing. When possible, use questions. There
are times when you need to use directives, but don't say things like "You need to
stop watching TV and talk with me," because that's setting up a power struggle.

Instead, try things like…

"Can I see your eyes?" (when trying to get them to look at you)

"We need to sit down and resolve our problem. Will you help me do that now?"

If your child or teen is upset, then please note: **The calmer you are, the calmer the child or teen will become.** It takes 2 to fuel a fight. If you aren't fighting, then he or she can blow off some steam, but there's nothing there to replenish it. If you raise your voice or stand over the child showing frustration or anger, the child will not de-escalate... however, you may scare the child into compliance... which, I HOPE is not your goal. If it is, please email me, because we have work to do!

Be physically lower than the child. If you are 5'2" and your adolescent is already taller than you are... MISSION ACCOMPLISHED! However, if you are addressing a child, and you are not a "Little Person" or in a wheelchair... PLEASE SIT DOWN ON A CHAIR, SOFA, BED, OR ON THE FLOOR. Standing over a child who is upset or who is ignoring you sends a confrontational message. Again, if the child is throwing objects or being hurtful, this does not apply, and you already HAVE his / her attention! In this case, it is appropriate for you to use a "polite, but firm" voice and say... **"THIS IS NOT OK, AND I NEED YOU TO SIT AND TALK TO ME."** You may have to be persistent, but remain calm and do not be intimidated. If your child sees fear in your eyes, or knows that you are intimidated by his / her behaviors, then those behaviors are working. Ironically, a child who uses intimidation does not WANT to be able to intimidate you. He / she is testing you to see if you:

1. Can remain calm and in control of yourself... meaning that you have the ability to handle a crisis, and therefore, they are SAFE in your care

2. Can see the behavior for what it is... a poor way of communicating feelings (rather than allowing yourself to be hurt by mean statements)

3. Will stay with the child or teen, or if you will leave him / her (as others may have in the past). **Some kids will try to push you away in order to make you prove your love, by not giving up on them.**

26

In implementing Honest Parenting, or ANY parenting style, it is important that your child not believe that he / she can intimidate you. If a child can intimidate a parent, then the child feels anxious and scared. Even though it may appear as though the child wants to be in control of YOU, he /she REALLY wants you to show that YOU are the wiser, more mature one, who is in control of your own emotions and behaviors... and that you recognize intimidation, manipulation, and "button pushing." Furthermore, he / she needs to know that you won't be sucked into having your "buttons pushed," or being manipulated!

You need a plan for dealing with any behavior or "test" that your child presents. Your first feeling of empowerment and stress relief will come from knowing how to handle any situation. I can help you to know what to say, what consequences to use, how to respond, and how to get your child or teen to follow through with your expectations. However, sometimes, the "plan" for certain behaviors includes help from a spouse or other relative. It's good for another person to let the child or teen know that it's not just YOU saying that the behavior is inappropriate, but that others think so, as well. Sometimes, help might be from a licensed therapist. Sometimes, unfortunately, it requires hospitalization or a residential facility.

 TIP!

Stating what you DO want the child to do, instead of what you want them to STOP DOING will give them a NEW BEHAVIOR to use. When a child is using a BEHAVIOR to communicate, rather than WORDS, it is partially because they can't think of an alternative. Your job is to GIVE them the alternate, "BETTER" behavior, so that they have something to START doing.

STEP 2: LET'S GET CLOSER!

The second step is to get close enough that the child cannot ignore you. If he / she is playing a video game, watching TV, trying to sleep, or otherwise not making eye contact…get in their personal space…in a "friendly" way. Sit on the floor. Do not put yourself in "the line of fire," if they are throwing objects or being hurtful. You are simply causing them to be aware of your presence, showing that you need their attention, and that you are not leaving or allowing them to continue playing in peace until they talk with you. That's right… talk "WITH" you… not "TO" you. You will have to be persistent… especially until they get used to you relating to them in this way, and until you show them several times that you will be there until they follow through with your expectation…. however long it takes. They will use whatever behaviors have gotten them their way in the past, so understand that as you use this technique several times, they will become familiar with "the drill," and will not test you as much. This gets easier and shorter as time goes on… as long as you remain consistent and DON'T GIVE UP!

EXAMPLE:

The TV Scenario:

In order for you to resolve a problem, the TV must be off. I mention this because it's a common source of a power struggle. The parent needs the child's attention and the child refuses to turn the TV off. So…the parent grabs the remote and turns it off. Then, the child goes to the TV and turns it back on. The parent unplugs it or uses the remote again. The child plugs it back in or turns it back on. What we have here is a POWER STRUGGLE. The best way to keep your child from ignoring you and not working through a problem is to stop their enjoyment of whatever is distracting them. So… if you sit right in front of the TV, your child can't see it… right? I'm not suggesting that you continue the power struggle by sitting between the child and the TV and then saying something like **"NOW**

who's winning? Huh??" You still want to be calm, use a calm voice, and say **"We really need to work this out, and watching TV right now is not OK. You can watch TV AFTER we work our problem out. YOU have control over how fast that can happen. Are you ready to start? Good. So, what do we both need to have before we start?"** Eventually, they will be able to answer you with something like… "calm voice… octopus arms… eye contact… paying attention…"

STEP 3: WORDS…NOT ACTIONS!

OK…now that you've established contact, here are some of the things that you need to be saying, in order to get your child ready to communicate. DO NOT BEGIN TO RESOLVE AN ISSUE UNTIL YOU AND YOUR CHILD HAVE THESE QUALITIES:

1. RELAXED, AND SITTING DOWN… and not playing with any toy, pet, or other object. However, if the object is not distracting the child, is not their way of defying the expectation that they do not play with anything while you are talking, and simply makes them feel secure, it's OK. Just be sure that they aren't manipulating and that they are truly able to maintain eye contact and to communicate well with you. If the object becomes a barrier, you need to wait for them to be able to put it down, out of reach.

2. EYE-CONTACT IS VERY IMPORTANT… You need to be looking at each other. This might be a process with a mistrusting child, but continually ask for their "Best Effort." For a child with low self-esteem, you may have to work on this, but they need to be facing you and not looking at anything else, such as a book.

3. CALM VOICE… If anyone begins to raise their voice, communication becomes less effective and needs to pause until everyone is calm again.

4. FOCUSED ON THE CONVERSATION BEFORE YOU BEGIN, AND ALL OF THE WAY THROUGH... You will most likely have to stop several times and ask the child what you just said... "Can you tell me in your own words what I just said?" or "Can you tell me in your own words what we just talked about?" It's important that they tell you in THEIR OWN words, so that you know that their mind processed the information and they aren't just being a "tape recorder" and repeating you.

Children and teens will test you to see if you really WILL wait until they decide to continue by meeting your expectation. They will play with objects, leave the room, want to fall asleep, and a host of other things... ANYTHING but sit with you and finish resolving the issue.

CONSISTENCY IS THE KEY! When you've been through these steps a few times, and the child knows that you WILL wait until they complete the steps, they will not test you as often or as hard. **PRAISE every little thing that they do correctly!** This goes a LONG way toward building your relationship and toward gaining their cooperation. If they know that you WANT them to succeed, then you're not the "big, mean parent," anymore. So...if they do a little better this time than they did the last, if they got halfway through resolving a problem before getting distracted, or any time that they use a calm voice or stop playing with a toy and focus on the conversation...say "THANKS!"

Try things like...

"Are your arms relaxed? Can you show me that they are limp, like an octopus or a wet noodle?"

"Can I see you sit down and stay in one place? Let's see if you can do that for 30 seconds. I'll time you. GREAT JOB!" (when they've done it, of course)

"Can I see your eyes?"

"Is your voice nice and soft?" "Where is your 'inside voice'?"

ASK QUESTIONS Why?

- Are QUESTIONS less confrontational than ORDERS, DEMANDS, or DIRECTIVES? YES!

- Do QUESTIONS make your child or teen THINK about what they are saying? YES!

- Do Questions cause your child or teen to learn by having to focus on the issue at hand, and by coming up with their own answers? YES!

- Do questions remove your child's or teen's tendency to "zone out," because they require involvement? YES!

- If you choose to GIVE STATEMENTS, instead of ASK QUESTIONS, can your child or teen just sit there until you're finished without really grasping what you're saying? YES!

- Do you want that? NO!

- Does having to think about answers to QUESTIONS cause your child or teen to be more prepared for relationships as adults? YES!

- Does having to think about answers to QUESTIONS cause your child or teen to be more introspective? YES!

- Are you thinking as you're reading these QUESTIONS? HOPEFULLY!

31

Instead of…

"Bryn, talking to your sister like that was the wrong thing to do."

(Which might make Bryn feel defensive, picked-on, and does nothing but state what YOU know)

Try…

"Bryn, if your sister spoke to you in that tone and said something similar to you, how would you feel?"

Or…

"Bryn, how do you think Chelsea feels after your conversation? Do you think that she's happy? Sad? If you put yourself in her place, how would you feel?"

Is ASKING QUESTIONS more effective in getting someone's attention?

OK… please remember that you don't need to use "sugary" words with adolescents as much. However, sometimes, they are effective in getting an adolescent to laugh… which is GREAT! If you can use words, gestures, or your tone of voice to get a teen to laugh, you are a step ahead! Please don't do it by making fun of them, though. They don't like that much. It's a "teen thing."

You may find that a child or teen will sit for a moment and then get up. You may find that they will be relaxed, and then escalate again. It is VERY important that you STOP the conversation whenever the he / she loses one of the requirements… calm voice, relaxed posture, focus on the conversation, sitting down… and some level of eye contact. If the child does not have all of these, he / she is either not "with you," or is TESTING you to see if they can get away with resolving the issue on their own terms and making you drop your expectations and give in, just to "get through it." Don't let them wear you down!

It's important that you wait until everyone involved in resolving the problem is ready. If something happens before school, for instance, and your child is calm enough to go to school, then as long as you address the issue before the end of the day, it should be alright to take them to school. There may be an instance where the child is very upset… or avoiding going to school on purpose. Obviously, if you can't transport the child safely, or if you can't get enough cooperation for the child or teen to be dressed and able to function in school, the problem must be resolved first. There may be times when you are late for work and your child or teen is late for school because of a problem. I feel for you on this one, and I know that you don't want to lose a job for being late. However, the faster you begin to use the steps to resolving a problem consistently, the sooner you will see progress!

As a therapist, I saw many occasions when kids would refuse to go to school. Sometimes, the problem might be worked out with only half of the school day left and the parent would sign them in. One incident lasted 14 hours. After that teen realized that her parents were not going to give up or give in, she relaxed, worked through the problem, and never had such a lengthy episode again. These things take time, but the progress is WELL worth it! And… the problems get smaller and shorter in duration as the child's communication skills and your relationship with them continue to improve.

Some of you will not entirely agree with what you are about to read. If you don't, it's perfectly OK. When you get to the end of this chapter just remember that we have something in common. We BOTH want your child or teen to make progress and for your family to be happy and stress-free.

So, whatever the true cause of your child's behavioral and emotional issues may be, the information and ideas in this book can help! It's not the source of the problem, but the cure that's most important.

ADD, ADHD, ODD, IED, CD and on, and on...

The following information is regarding children and teens who have been diagnosed with ADD, ADHD, as well as ODD (Oppositional Defiant Disorder), Intermittent Explosive Disorder, Conduct Disorder and several others. While the symptoms of each diagnosis are different, many of these are not chemical or biological issues, but BEHAVIORAL and EMOTIONAL issues.

A mental health diagnosis is simply a name given to a list of symptoms. It helps us to understand what a person's behaviors and issues might be like, without having to describe each one. If someone says "I've been diagnosed with ADHD," you might get a picture of someone who fidgets, has trouble following through with a task, is hyperactive, and jumps from one topic of conversation to another (just for example). So, ADHD is a lot faster to say or type than a full description, much like we all know what the color blue looks like, without having to explain that it's the color of the sky on a clear day, or of Aunt Elsie's eyes.

Let's not get too caught up in diagnoses or labels, because if a child or teen thinks that being given a diagnosis means that they have a permanent condition that they can't overcome or improve upon, they may give up. Also, if a person believes in taking medicine for "permanent, biological" issues, then they will be likely to believe that they have no control over the issues, and that they will be dependent on medicines forever. That's not a good place to be emotionally, or physically. Your child's or teen's liver will thank you for not looking at medicine as a cure, but realizing that, while it can be a temporary tool, to keep anxiety and hyperactivity under control as you actually work with the child or teen on the issues and empower him or her to make real progress... **medicine does not cure emotional issues. It only masks them.**

34

Now, there are some real biological and chemical conditions that can cause behavioral and emotional issues. For example, if your teen has epilepsy, then he or she might be very self-conscious about it. They may be introverted, depressed, scared and angry that they have this problem… especially if they don't completely understand what it is, and how it will affect their life. So, the biological condition of epilepsy might cause them to make poor choices in their behavior. It might cause them to yell, curse, become withdrawn, throw objects, and even do drugs. It all depends on the person, their personality, and other circumstances… such as the level of support that they have from their family, friends, and doctor.

There are a number of other biological issues that can also cause a child or teen to be angry and frustrated, depressed, etc. My point is this… Treat MEDICAL conditions with MEDICINE (and also emotional support). Treat EMOTIONAL and BEHAVIORAL issues by working with the child or teen on these issues. Only use medicines if ABSOLUTELY NECESSARY, AND ONLY FOR AS LONG AS IT TAKES TO MAKE ENOUGH PROGRESS WITH THE CHILD OR TEEN TO GET THEM UNDER ENOUGH CONTROL TO LEARN AND BE SAFE.

So…no matter what you "NAME THE PAIN"… the answer is STILL the same…Honest Parenting. Use the steps to resolving problems that are listed in this book. Learn them, and get your WHOLE family SOOOO used to using them that you all know them by heart…because the child or teen that you're trying to make progress with will be likely to have conflicts with all family members. And… you can use these steps for conflicts that DON'T involve the child or teen that you're focusing on… because they work for EVERYONE! You can also use them when your child or teen has a problem with a friend, with someone in school, or in the community. Using the steps to resolving a problem with a neighbor, whose window your child broke with a baseball, or with a store owner, whom your child stole some candy from can be a GREAT step! I've even been asked to adapt Honest Parenting for use by employers with their employees. So it's important to understand that this is an effective way to resolve problems for anyone, no matter how old they are and no matter whether they are dealing with a family member, or someone else.

About ADD and ADHD…

If your child has ever been diagnosed with ADD (ATTENTION DEFICIT DISORDER) or ADHD (ATTENTION DEFICIT HYPERACTIVITY DISORDER), then PLEASE read this section. I want to preface the next few paragraphs by letting you know that I have GREAT respect for all of the good, sincere, compassionate mental health professionals and educators of the world. There are MANY helpful, hard-working, teachers, principals, counselors, therapists, social workers, Psychologists, and Psychiatrists whose contributions to the lives of children and families are PRICELESS! I've been fortunate to know some, and have had teachers and professors to whom I will be eternally grateful.

DEFINITIONS:

PSYCHIATRIST: A MEDICAL DOCTOR (MD) who deals with patients who are diagnosed with mental disorders, and treats them, primarily, with medication.

PSYCHOLOGIST: A NON-MEDICAL DOCTOR (Usually PhD., Psy.D, or Ed.D) who deals with patients diagnosed with mental disorders and treats them using a treatment plan, which consists of testing, talking, exercises, assignments, and building a relationship with them, so that they can work together. They try to find the source of an emotional or relational issue or problem and create a plan to correct it. They may work with the child, and with family members.

THERAPIST: The same idea as a PSYCHOLOGIST, but usually has a Master's Degree, rather than a Doctorate. (Usually MS, MSW, or LPC)

SOCIAL WORKER: Practices therapy or treatment much like a PSYCHOLOGIST or THERAPIST. Like a PSYCHOLOGIST or THERAPIST, they use non-medical means to address the emotional development of the child and family dynamics. (Usually MSW, MS, BSW, or BA)

The primary symptom of ADD is inability to focus or concentrate on a task for an extended period of time. This usually leads to unfinished tasks and disorganization. It can also affect schoolwork. ADHD is ADD with an added symptom of hyperactivity… meaning that the person may fidget, have difficulty sitting still (or sitting at all), have bursts of energy, and move about frequently. Both of these conditions include daydreaming, and many children who have been diagnosed with them are intelligent and creative.

Can your child or teen watch a 30-minute or hour-long TV show? Can they play a video game or a board game for half an hour? Can they put together a jigsaw puzzle with more than 10 pieces? If so, then they DO have the ability to concentrate! There is a very good chance that they are using "selective attention / inattention" to focus only on things that interest them… EVEN IF THEY AREN'T AWARE THAT THEY'RE DOING THIS! If this is the case, then they have a behavioral issue that involves lack of self-discipline and delaying gratification. They choose not to focus on things that they SHOULD focus on… because those things aren't interesting or fun to them. Please consider this test, if your child has been diagnosed with "ADD or ADHD." SOLVE the problem. Don't be so quick to mask the symptoms and possibly damage your child's body and self-esteem with medication. Help them to become happy, productive adults, rather than someone with low self-esteem, who thinks that they are limited in what they can accomplish because of some illness that they will always have to take medication for.

What if I told you that I've never seen a single child who was diagnosed with ADD or ADHD and didn't have another, perfectly logical reason for acting the way that they did? What if I told you that there are doctors and pharmaceutical companies making fortunes on pumping kids full of drugs that could have serious, long-term side effects? What if I told you that some teachers and principals encourage parents to have their children see doctors in the hopes that they will be placed on medication… thereby making them easier to "handle" at school? What if I told you that labeling a kid with a "diagnosis," "condition," "mental illness," or "disease," can damage their self esteem FOREVER and can seriously affect their emotional wellbeing and their level of success in life? What if I told you that many children who have to go to doctors and take medication feel that they are somehow "inferior," or "different," or "sick"?

Who am I to say that DOCTORS could possibly be wrong, since they have learned so much to earn their degrees? Could those doctors have simply had a bad theory? Could they be anxious to make money from having more clients? Could they want prominence by having their studies published? Could they be under pressure from professionals who deal with these kids and frustrated parents because it's more convenient to create a diagnosis for symptoms and to mask the symptoms with drugs than to do the work that it takes to actually SOLVE the problem? Could they just plain... be wrong? Hysteria was also once thought to be a medical condition. If you remember, for centuries, people thought that the world was flat. Do you ever wonder why we didn't have ADD and ADHD in the 1950's, 1960's, or 1970's? In fact, it wasn't really until the 1990's that it became "popular." So... how, did we suddenly begin to produce children with this disorder that has been reported as being "biological, chemical, or biochemical"? Hmmmm……

I'm not slamming Psychiatrists. Some are VERY good! Just make sure that you have one of the GOOD ones, if you use one. Make sure that you feel as though the Psychiatrist (or any other professional) has your child's best interest at heart. The goal is to try EVERYTHING... including Honest Parenting, before resorting to medication. Medication should be your LAST resort, and when you have an EMOTIONAL or BEHAVIORAL issue, you can almost always resolve it with an EMOTIONAL and BEHAVIORAL solution.

It's easier to give pills to kids than it is to do the work that actually helps the child to learn better behaviors and self-control. How are Psychiatrists and other medical doctors trained to deal with problems? They are trained to prescribe medication. Some of them will look at other measures, but their primary function is to send a patient to the pharmacy with a prescription. I do not believe that the symptoms that make up the "disorders" ADD and ADHD are usually medical issues, but emotional and behavioral issues. If your child has been "accused" of having "ADD or ADHD" or if they have been diagnosed by a Psychiatrist, then I would suggest that you read some of the books that have been published questioning the validity of these diagnoses as being chemical imbalances or biological in nature. And… get a second opinion. Also make sure that your child doesn't eat too much sugar or too many carbohydrates! Please read on for more possible causes of these symptoms.

EXAMPLE:

Let's say that you have insomnia. You can hardly get to sleep. You only sleep about 2-3 hours each night, when you finally DO fall asleep. So, you see your doctor, who prescribes one of the popular sleeping medications. It helps you to sleep. If you watch commercials for some of the medications that are being marketed through television, you will see that some of them have scary side effects. "Stop using this pill if you have heart palpitations, if your vision becomes impaired, or if you suddenly begin to bleed from your ears as your head explodes." OK, slight exaggeration, but really… listen to some of these commercials, and you'll want to do research on any medication that your child or teen is taking. How are these even LEGAL?

So… your sleeping pills work, and you can now get 7 or 8 hours of sleep each night…as long as you continue taking them…which makes you dependent on them (which continues to make money for the doctor and for the pharmaceutical company, by the way). It's OK… with malpractice insurance so high and the good intentions that most of them have, most doctors DESERVE to make money. I'm also in favor of pharmaceutical companies developing life-saving medications. There are many medications that have made us well, relieved our pain, and saved our lives or the lives of our family members.

Now, let's say that I take the same sleeping pill that you take. I don't have insomnia. I sleep well every night. But, I take the same pill. What will happen? Will it still have an effect on me? Will I fall asleep faster? YOU BET! So… if you give a child medication for "ADD or ADHD," it doesn't matter that they may not have a chemical imbalance or some biological "problem" that causes the behavior… they will often be calmer and "act better," because of a drug. Does that mean that the drug is correcting a chemical imbalance, or just that it's altering his / her mood and sedating him / her?

All drugs have side effects, and they affect people differently. I might be in favor of a drug with minor (known) short-term side effects that was taken **TEMPORARILY**, so that a child could be calm enough and focused enough to learn new behaviors and to make behavioral progress. However, many doctors have no planned timeframe or a method of actually solving the problem. A time-limited combination of medication and parents (and sometimes, a therapist) working with a child on controlling impulses and increasing ability to focus on tasks (and follow through with them), is sometimes the best answer.

It's DANGEROUS to allow someone to believe that they have a "mental disorder"… to make them think that they are "weird," "ill," or "sick." Yet, when they begin taking PILLS or SHOTS because they need to "act better," and when they become a "patient," the damage to their self-esteem begins.

If we treat behavioral and emotional issues with drugs, we will have generations of adults who are emotionally underdeveloped, incompetent, and unable to become independent, productive people. Again… we will simply be covering the symptoms and not solving the problem. Please be aware of the following 4 causes of behaviors that are often seen as "ADD or ADHD."

REASON 1: ABUSE

Many of the children whom I've worked with have encountered abuse. What happens when a child is yelled at, belittled, called names, made to feel unworthy or inferior? What happens when a child is hit, locked in a closet, deprived of food, or sent to his / her room for hours? What happens when a child is sexually abused?

Can you imagine being small and weak, and so afraid of someone that you can't think of anything else, but... when is the NEXT time I'll be hurt? Will he / she be there when I get home from school? Will it happen again tonight? Can you imagine waking up every day wishing that you would die? Can you imagine going to sleep at night wishing that the person who was abusing you would die? Can you imagine going to school and trying to concentrate on what the teacher is saying or writing on the board when all you can think about is how you were trying to go to sleep last night and someone crept into your room and did terrible things to you? Can you imagine trying to take a spelling test when you know that you'll be hit, yelled at, and sent to your room when you get home because you forgot to put your cereal bowl in the sink this morning? Can you imagine being afraid to even GO to school because when you go to the restroom or dress out for PE, the other kids make fun of you, harass you, call you names, threaten you, or beat you up?

These scenarios are reality for TOO MANY children. And... I've not begun to describe them in enough detail for them to have their full impact. Your child may have been abused without your knowledge. Or, like one child I've known, they may be continually abused by a certain relative once or twice each year... only on holidays.

Abuse can cause a child to be anxious, unfocused, and unable to concentrate. It can also cause fidgeting, hyperactivity, and inability to stay still. Beyond that, in younger children, they may be destructive and completely out of control. If abuse occurs at an early age, a child will use behaviors (rather than words) to show fear and anxiety. Abuse can also cause the creativity that many diagnosed children have. Their fragile minds use creativity as an escape from the horrific thoughts that

41

want to creep into their days and nights. Additionally, abused kids can become exceptionally intelligent, because they HAVE to, in order to learn to survive and to protect themselves.

It is very rare that a child or teen will feel comfortable enough to freely tell someone that they are being abused. Often, they are ashamed, made to feel that it is their fault, are being threatened, or are afraid that they will not be believed.

HOW OFTEN DO CHILDREN MAKE UP STORIES ABOUT BEING ABUSED? ALMOST NEVER!

REASON 2: TRAUMA

Has your child been in a terrible auto accident or a fire? Has your child been seriously injured in another type of accident? Has your child lost a parent or sibling? Has your child witnessed a violent crime, such as a robbery, mugging, or rape? Has your child witnessed domestic violence?

Any of these things and many more traumatic possibilities can cause anxiety, and fleeting thoughts. Not being able to concentrate because of "shellshock" or "Posttraumatic Stress Disorder" can also appear as the commonly recognized symptoms of "ADD and ADHD."

REASON 3: DISORGANIZED, HYPERACTIVE, OR UNFOCUSED CARETAKERS

Here's one that I've seen many, many times. I'm guessing that some of you have a little trouble of your own with completing tasks, focusing on a subject or topic, etc. If you think that YOU might have some symptoms of "ADD or ADHD," then remember that kids learn by example and experience. If you are anxious or disorganized, then they are likely to be, as well. Kids learn to speak with accents similar to their parents. They often walk with the same gate that their parents have. They learn to tie their shoes, make sandwiches, and make a bed in the manner that their parents do. So... if you have more advanced and controlled symptoms of losing focus, being late, not being organized, etc., then your child could simply be learning from you. If you are disorganized and unfocused, how could your child learn to be organized and focused? Where would they get those skills? They DO learn from you... the good, and the bad.

The answer to this is to work on your own issues, while you help your child or teen. Your child might be the perfect motivation that you need to do so. This doesn't mean that you're a "bad parent." It just means that your child may not have some "mental disorder" that they will be labeled with and have to live down for the rest of their lives! They might just need to unlearn some bad habits and learn NEW behaviors to replace the ones that don't work for them.

REASON 4: SELECTIVE ATTENTION / INATTENTION

In this scenario, a child simply pays attention to things that are fun or interesting, and daydreams or tunes out things that aren't fun or interesting. The child will not always do this on purpose, and will not necessarily know that they are doing it. As in a previous paragraph in this chapter, you might try watching your child to see if they can focus on a TV show, movie, jigsaw puzzle, video game, or an activity... such as kickball, or another sport that they enjoy. If your child can do this for 30 minutes, an hour... or more, then it's likely that their problem can be corrected by bringing the issue to their attention and working with them on focusing. Help them complete short tasks, and celebrate each one. Redirect them, gently, back to the task at hand. Sit with them and help them to complete homework. Gentle prompting and supervision, to ensure that they stay on task, will help them... especially when they know that you are really trying to help, and are not frustrated with their learning issue. If they are opposed to close supervision, make that their motivation for becoming more independent! Let them know that when they are able to show you that they can complete a task WITHOUT you watching, then you won't have to watch them so closely. Focus on short tasks, first, and help them to work toward longer, more complicated tasks. Start with a 10-minute cleanup of their bedroom, or helping you fold laundry. Work toward vacuuming a room, or raking the yard. Of course, homework will be a good one to work on, as well!

The bottom line here is that YOU **CAN** HELP YOUR CHILD OR TEEN! YOU can help them to become happy, respectful, responsible, productive, independent adults…often without medication, or with medication on a temporary basis. YOU have the POWER! You just need time, dedication, patience, energy, and knowledge. And…the help of your family would be nice, too! Remember that ADD and ADHD are not scary "diseases," just names for lists of symptoms.

NOTES:

CHAPTER 4

What HASN'T WORKED... and WHY?

If yelling, spanking, time-outs, take-aways, bribery, or anything else you've tried REALLY worked...
you wouldn't be reading this now.

Rewards and punishments do not work in the long run. Why?

Rewards teach children that they will be "paid" for good behavior. In life, we are not PAID to do the "right thing." Do we get personal satisfaction from doing the right thing? HOPEFULLY! But, we don't get paid extra for getting to work on time, for not being criminals, etc. We usually just don't have NEGATIVE consequences, if we "do the right thing." So... if you give children money, a toy, or anything else in exchange for good behavior, they begin to think that they should be PAID for being good people. Also, they learn that they can use NEGATIVE behaviors as a threat or as leverage to get you to give them things. What a NIGHTMARE that sets up! NO MAKING DEALS!

If you want to give your child a toy, or their favorite dinner, or some money... do it "just because you LOVE them"... NOT because you are PAYING them for doing something that they should do, anyway.

Punishments (like grounding) do not work, because they cause a child to fear parents, not to trust them, and to want to get away with things… just hiding their mischief better, so that they don't get caught the next time.

Punishment drives a wedge between a parent and a child. If you are using punishment of any kind, please pay close attention to the information on LOGICAL and NATURAL CONSEQUENCES. These will replace "punishment."

If you use rewards and punishment, you are not instilling in your child or teen the idea of doing what's right "because they are a good person and should get satisfaction and pride from doing good." Instead, you are teaching them that "When I do what my parent wants, I get money, toys or privileges. When I don't, I get punished. So, THAT'S why I do the right thing… not because I'm a good person." Do you see my point? If someone is only "good" when you are there to give them something, or if they refrain from bad behavior only to avoid punishment, then what will they do when you're not there to watch them? It's a LOT of work on your part to keep them in line, and also gives you no plan for when they become adults and you CAN'T watch over them.

Yelling and hitting or spanking… The short version is that these don't work because they don't replace the inappropriate behavior with an appropriate behavior that your child can use in the future. Also, they cause a child to be fearful of the parent, and not to trust them… not to mention that they teach the child to yell and hit when THEY are mad… something that can get them in trouble at school and in the community. More on these, later in this chapter.

Time-Out… Why do we put a child in time-out? To let them calm down? To let them think about what they've done wrong? To give ourselves a break? OK, again… they don't learn a NEW behavior that can replace whatever they did wrong. Also, what happens at the end of the time-out if they aren't calm yet? Do you just let them sit there all day and become more restless? If you did, would it really accomplish anything? Is the goal for the child to be in time-out all of the time and to feel badly about himself / herself, OR… is the goal to be able to go through the day, participating in the activities and work successfully?

Take-Aways… Taking things away from a child or teen when they make poor choices doesn't work because it makes the parent "the bad guy," and doesn't teach a new behavior that the kid can use the next time that they are in a similar situation. It also associates their behavior with toys, an MP3 player, a video game, a bicycle, etc. Their behavior has nothing to do with these things, unless these objects were involved in the incident. EXCEPTION: If a child goes too far away from the house on his / her bike and you've already physically shown him / her the boundaries, then not riding the bike for a day is appropriate. You need to let him / her try again, though, in a day… not a week. The goal is not punishment. It's to offer chances to succeed. A LOGICAL CONSEQUENCE is a consequence of making a poor choice that…

1. You implement
2. Is closely related to the poor choice
3. Gives the child another chance to look forward to
4. Happens within 24 hours of the incident

We need to cause the child or teen to focus on what he / she did wrong and a better choice to make, rather than on how mean the PARENT is being. A child or teen learns faster if positive and negative consequences are immediate. If your child consistently goes outside the boundary on his / her bike, then every other day, they have a chance to show you that they can ride within the boundary. If they stay within the boundary, then they can ride the next day. If they don't, it'll be the day after tomorrow before they can try again. They will get the message much more quickly, if the cycle of making a choice and then having a positive or negative consequence, based on their choice, is short. They will see that THEY have control. This isn't about "doing what I say," it's about safety, a child building trust with you, learning to stay within limits, and recognizing that the child is in control of his / her own behavior, which leads to more freedom…or less freedom.

Bribery… I've seen a LOT of parents and grandparents use this one! Some of you wouldn't DREAM of it, but others have definitely made "deals" with kids to "Be good and I'll buy you dinner from McDonald's." "Stop your tantrum and I'll buy you that toy." It's obvious that you can go broke doing this, but even making deals for things that don't cost money (like letting them stay up past their bedtime)… don't work. Why? It puts the kid in control when they aren't ready for it, and they are using inappropriate behaviors to get what they want. What if they have to wait in line at the grocery, at a bank, or in traffic when they grow up? What if their teacher or their friend's mom doesn't give them what they want and they explode? In school or in the community, this will get them in trouble.

Sure… bribery may get you out of the store without embarrassment, or it might keep you from having to deal with a problem when you're tired. But, in the long run, you're not doing your child or yourself any favors if you bribe them. It's VERY important for a child not to associate privileges, toys, clothes or money with how much you love them or with the quality of your relationship. Do you know an adult who equates what their paramour or spouse BUYS them with how much they LOVE them? Do you know someone who is superficial and OBSESSED with brand name items that seem to give them their self-esteem? This is a person who might say "I know how much he / she loves me by what I get for Valentine's Day." They were a kid, once! SOOOO sad! BLING is NOT LOVE! It's NICE, but it's NOT LOVE!

Also… if you bribe a 3 year-old, candy, an ice cream cone, or a cheap toy will usually do the trick. When they become 12 or 13, a CD, magazine… or maybe a trip to the skating rink might work. Later, it becomes an MP3 Player, an expensive shirt, a car, or who knows what? As kids grow older, they only become bigger, stronger, and smarter… and they want more expensive things! So… save yourself the difficulty of dealing with a 16 year-old who has 3 year-old tantrums and as Barney Fife would say… "Nip it in the bud!" (Nicely!)

A NOTE on YELLING, HITTING, and SPANKING,…

It may FEEL natural for some of us to yell when we get mad… but that's only because we are in that habit and have done it for years. This is a habit that needs to be broken. Yelling and hitting are learned behaviors. They are usually passed from one generation to another. To stop the pattern, a person who does these things has to make a decision to take a step forward and learn a different way of relating to people. If you yell or hit, who yelled at you? Who hit you? You have a chance to stop the cycle. THAT is a TRULY powerful thing!

Not everyone yells and hits. Some do only one, and some do neither. Still, they are both abusive and harmful to a relationship. Some people cry, some "stew quietly," and some withdraw. Kids (and adults with underdeveloped communication skills), sometimes become destructive. If your child punches holes in walls, for instance, learn how to patch them and keep the materials and tools handy. Repairing the hole is a logical consequence and a relationship building activity that teaches a kid to take responsibility. You may do most of the work, but it's the activity that counts. THEN… work with them on using WORDS to express anger or frustration, instead of punching walls. We're working with baby steps, so even yelling or cursing is better than being hurtful or destructive.

When WE yell or hit, we teach our kids to do it, too! By doing things that are inappropriate or ineffective, we send the message to kids that it's OK.

 "Do as I say, not as I do" never worked, because we can TELL children that… but if they see us doing something, they will learn it and will imitate us… even without trying. Also, when we "raise our voices," it still may SOUND like yelling to someone smaller. From a child's perspective, we are BIG! So…everything we do is exaggerated. A visibly upset parent can be SCARY to a child.

We are more likely to yell when a child pushes our buttons. So…learn to recognize when a child is pushing your "buttons" and to not let it work!
If a child can push your buttons and annoy you into yelling…Who is in control of whom? Yelling is a choice, and it's a GREAT idea to choose talking, instead! Yelling is just a more-sophisticated temper tantrum.

By the same token, using a calm voice and setting GOOD examples of how we want kids to communicate with us will send a POSITIVE message, and they will use THOSE behaviors, too! It takes practice to change. We can get better and better at catching ourselves when we're about to yell or lose our cool… and at taking a few minutes to calm ourselves before we continue the conversation. That's the SAME skill that we want our kids to learn!

If we hit, then so might our child.

When I talk about hitting, well…there are 2 kinds. One is considered "abuse" by most people. The other is spanking (and some people take that to an abusive level, as well). Now, my parents spanked me several times… a couple with a belt, some

53

with their hands, and my mom used to have me break off a switch from a bush in our yard. Love my Mom. Don't miss the bush. So, I understand very well what spanking is about for parents. It's been done for generations and many people who were spanked believe that they turned out very well... myself, included. Fortunately, my parents abandoned spanking and used some of the ideas in this book with me. And, they were also very nurturing, in combination with setting firm limits. If you have spanked your child, it doesn't mean you're a "bad parent". It just means that you used something that doesn't work.

Also, spanking truly does no good at all in teaching a child what they need to do differently the next time they are faced with making a positive choice or a poor choice in their behavior. It causes a child to fear their parent, and destroys trust. Beyond that, it sends the message that "it's OK to hit others when I'm mad." Spanking is a punishment, and often comes from anger or a desire to control. Neither of those traits are positive or healthy. We are focusing on TEACHING a child to make better choices... not scaring them into submission. How you relate to a child has everything to do with who and what they become when they grow up. Life experiences will make them strong enough, without you hitting them.

Even if you don't think that the responses that I've mentioned in this chapter are inappropriate, we can at least agree that they don't work.

If you haven't seen an episode of "Leave it to Beaver," lately, then it's a good idea to check your TV schedule. Ward Cleaver (the father), played by Hugh Beaumont, was a very calm, cool, and collected parent, most of the time. There were a few moments of disappointment or disgust with his kids' behavior, and even then, he was able to express it in a caring, concerned way... and still let them know that he was angry or disappointed in them. I'm not examining the actual consequences that he implemented... which were usually things like "being grounded," but his caring, and not overly emotional, demeanor is a GREAT example to follow. June (the mother, played by Barbara Billingsley) did a fine job, also... but usually referred the kids to their father for discipline. That may have been par for the course back then, but I strongly encourage caretakers in two-parent households to communicate with each other, to be present when problems are being worked out, and to share Honest Parenting with each other. In therapeutic terms, this is called a "unified front." It means that the child or teen hears the same things and gets the same responses from both caretakers. He / she knows that the parents agree on issues and communicate with each other. It makes the child or teen know that they can't play one parent against the other, and removes any confusion about what the "right way to do things" is.

There are children who will seem to LIKE the fact that they can hurt you, either physically, or by hurting your feelings. These are usually children who have been abused, and who have very little, if any conscience. Conscience will develop as you nurture them and provide structure and logical and natural consequences. **You can help by showing your sensitivity, by being a good role model… and by not being afraid to say "I'm sorry" when you make a mistake. Remember, they learn from example, and admitting YOUR mistakes will make them feel better about admitting THEIRS. Also, smiles, laughter, and a pat on the back or a hug go a LONG WAY!**

NOTES:

CHAPTER 5
COMMUNICATION

A lot of time is wasted by parents trying to talk with their kids and their words "going in one ear and out the other," as my parents would say. I'll show you how to communicate in such a way that you're heard, and won't have the frustrating feeling of not being "listened to." In this chapter, we'll explore the difference between communicating with behaviors and communicating with words. Throughout the book, please pay attention to body language, tone of voice, and eye contact, which are all important to communication. The expectations of communicating go for EVERYONE! Kids need to be understood, too.

It's important that you be specific when communicating with your child. "Be good," "listen to me," or other general terms don't tell a child much, and therefore, you may request something that is difficult to follow... setting the child up to fail. Also, use words that express how you feel. Moms and Dads, you have to be able to use words to communicate your feelings and requests to a child before he / she can learn from you how to express feelings verbally.

Here's how communication starts...

EXAMPLE:

If you allow an inappropriate behavior to get a child what they want, then they will continue to use that behavior! When a baby cries, we feed the baby, change the diaper, hold the baby... go through a series of guesses to "fix" the problem and cause the baby to stop crying. We "cater" to the baby. So, learning to talk is a lot of work for a baby to do, when its needs are being met simply by crying.

However, as we keep talking to the baby and asking questions like… Do you want the bottle? Are you sleepy? Is it nap time? The baby catches on to words like "bottle," which might come out "baba" or for my brother, "sleepy" came out "seep." The reasons that babies begin to use words are… your repetition and teaching, and because THEY WORK FASTER! If a baby can say "baba," then he / she doesn't have to wait for you to guess what he / she wants! INSTANT GRATIFICATION! (Just what MICROWAVES, ATM's and CELL PHONES give to adults!) Waiting in line at the bank, or using an oven instead of a microwave are equal to a baby waiting for you to guess what he or she wants… UN-FUN!

This, Moms and Dads, is what we can use as motivation for your kids to take MORE "baby steps" and to begin using WORDS, instead of BEHAVIORS to get what they want. We also want them to be able to accept NOT always getting what they want, whether it's a toy, your immediate attention, or to be first in line.

A child who does not learn to communicate effectively becomes frustrated and does not get his / her needs met. So, inappropriate behaviors occur, and often, trouble with peer relations, school, and certainly, with the family. Of course, if a child has hearing loss, for instance, he / she may need to have that addressed, and the communication skills may develop more quickly. That's why hearing and eyesight testing is important in diagnosing problems.

If your child is using behaviors to show frustration, ask them to use WORDS! A child who is in the habit of using behaviors to communicate may need consistent prompting, in order to begin talking more. This is no reflection on your child's intelligence. We learn to use new behaviors by DOING them, and if we are on a learning curve, we need reminders. So, ASK them to use words, set the EXPECTATION that they use words… and they just might!

Use words that your child will understand, and that express how you feel …

"You really push my buttons, sometimes!"

"Sometimes, I get frustrated with your behaviors!"

"If you want my help or attention, I need you to use a calm voice."

"I feel sad when we have arguments."

"Sometimes, your words and behaviors hurt my feelings."

STOPPING THE VICIOUS CYCLE

(Getting Your Child or Teen Out of a "RUT")

Often, you may find that when your child or teen begins to raise their voice, escalate to a high level of agitation, demonstrate their low frustration tolerance, show inability to delay gratification... have a TANTRUM... they just can't seem to STOP! It's like they are on a downward spiral and just can't come out of the mood that they're in and start to calm down. Here are a few things that can help you to de-escalate them and to teach them about the difference between "wearing their heart on their sleeves" and just expressing every thought that comes through their minds and looking at the big picture... their goal...what they REALLY WANT... what they're hoping to accomplish.

EXAMPLE:

There's a teenager who plays basketball for her high school team. She is liked by the other girls on the team. She tries to be a team player and generally has a positive attitude, as basketball lifts her self-esteem and is her only serious hobby or activity. She is just as dedicated and as good a player as any of the girls on the team. However, she is a little hyperactive and impulsive at times... meaning that when she's frustrated, she "uses words" to express that... sometimes loudly enough for the coach to hear... things that might better be left unsaid, in order for to her reach her goal of getting more playing time.

The coach has some favorites on the team. Some of the girls play more than others. Some get more help from the coach, when they ask for one-on-one coaching or advice. The coach seems not to be overly interested in making the girls "the best players that they can be." In other words, the coach will teach basketball to the extent of offering the girls information on how to play, but the girls are on their own as far as learning to be a team, improving on their individual skills, and really getting something out of the season that will make them into better players. Needless to say, it's not as fun and positive an experience as this teenager would like for it to be.

So, you can imagine the teens frustration. Also, her mother isn't terribly pleased, because she wants her daughter to be happy and to have every opportunity to excel. Not to mention that there are tournaments which the family travels to, at their own expense, and the girl's mother sometimes takes days off of work for these. So, the total investment of time and money doesn't seem to give this teen or her family much of a return. Driving 3 hours and staying in a hotel to watch her daughter sit on the sidelines for 2 days, and then driving back doesn't seem like a satisfying way for a parent to spend a weekend, does it? On the bright side, there is an opportunity for some good bonding time in the car, though.

So... while the Mom is upset about the situation, she is more able to use self-control, think of different ways to possibly resolve the problem, and not say things to the coach, impulsively, which would worsen the situation.

The teen, on the other hand, not having as much restraint, has, occasionally, muttered a few thoughts which were overheard, shot a few piercing glances, and shown with posture and body language that she was unhappy. The coach views this as "having a bad attitude."

After almost every practice and almost every game, our teen would begin venting her frustration to her mother as soon as she got into the car to go home. Why is this GOOD?

1. She wasn't venting in front of other players or the coach.

2. She was using WORDS instead of BEHAVIORS, such as throwing the ball hard against the bleachers, stomping around, etc.

But, will it RESOLVE the problem... not quite. It just became a vicious cycle that would never end, because the real issues weren't being dealt with.

Taking her mother's suggestion, the teen did go to the coach one evening, after practice, and sincerely ask for individual help. She didn't receive the warm response that she was hoping for. So, that evening, she felt as though she had tried the "right way" of doing things, and still didn't get what she wanted. At a loss for what to do next, she resorted to behaviors that had worked for her when she was younger. Here's what happened...

Our teen had many, MANY negative comments about the coach in the car, on her way home. It was basically a 30-minute venting session. Her mother agreed that she should be upset. She tried to calm her daughter down by validating her feelings. Rather than just being able to "get it all out," this time, our teen worked herself into a full-blown state of being loud and angry, and the adrenaline rush didn't help matters any. She got home, threw her gym bag and shoes as she walked in... breaking a vase and knocking over her brother's soda, which made a dark spot on the light beige carpet. When her mother tried to switch from being a listener and validating the girl's feelings to being in charge of the household and letting the girl know that it was OK to be upset, but not OK to throw things, break the case, or spill the soda, our teen escalated more...

"YOU HATE ME, TOO!"

"YOU CARE ABOUT YOUR VASE AND YOUR CARPET MORE THAN ME!"

And, so… what began as a simple conversation between mother and daughter, allowing the daughter to vent her frustration with the coach, and her mother validating her feelings and being an understanding listener, on her side of the issue… escalated into an episode at home.

Our teen wouldn't calm down. She slammed the door to her room, called a friend on her cell phone and vented to her for a few minutes, and continued to stomp around the house cursing the coach, and now… her Mom.

In response, her Mom gathers herself, reminds herself that the things that her daughter said were only an immature release of frustration and that she shouldn't take them personally, pictured in her mind how cute her daughter was, as a baby, and begins to use the 4 steps to resolving a problem (those are in another chapter, and are closely related to this chapter).

She nicely… and in a voice that's almost EXCITED… lets her daughter know that she has some ideas on how they can resolve the issue with the coach, but that first, she needs to clean the soda from the carpet with paper towels, carpet cleaner, and the vacuum, and we need to figure out how she can replace the vase… which, fortunately, wasn't terribly precious or expensive.

Telling her daughter that she had ideas on how to resolve the problem with the coach, was what got the de-escalation started. When a kid is in despair, letting them know that there might be an ANSWER to what is upsetting them is sometimes what can turn things around.

And so, the daughter is still very upset, and at first, says…

"THERE'S NO ANSWER. WHAT SHOULD I DO… KILL HER?"

So, her Mom says to her…

As soon as we can get this soda cleaned and work out a way to replace the vase, we can really concentrate on this and I think that we can do a few things to make things better for you.

Mom is calm. Mom is sitting down. Mom is the one with the answers, who is just waiting for her daughter to de-escalate, because Mom is not arguing with her. No fight = no continued escalation. Mom also realizes that even if the vase WAS expensive, or had sentimental value, her DAUGHTER is more important.

The daughter sits in a living room chair and they begin to talk. Mom's words are in **BOLD BLUE**, and her daughter's words are in quotation marks.

"OK, what's next. Can I just deal with the carpet and the vase later and talk about the coach?"

I know that you're anxious to find an answer that will get this basketball thing resolved, but we really need to work out the vase and the carpet things first. It'll only take a few minutes, and then we'll get right to basketball. You can be patient! I know, because I've seen you do it before!

 TIP!

Once you get your child or teen to do something GOOD, like lower their voice, demonstrate patience, de-escalate from a tantrum, etc. then you can USE that example FOREVER, to remind them that they CAN do it again!

"OK, let's just get this over with. While I'm cleaning the carpet, what do I have to do to replace the vase? I don't even know where you got it."

Well, how about a choice? It could come out of your chore money, and we could see if Target still has one, or something similar. Or, you could clean the kitchen for me this weekend.

"I'll clean the kitchen. That way I can use my money to go to a movie."

OK, fair enough. Now, what day would you like to clean the kitchen… Saturday, or Sunday?

"I'll do it Sunday."

OK, but I'd really appreciate it if you'd start early in the day, because you need rest for school on Monday, and I see some potential for a rough night if you have to stay up late to get it done well. What time will you be able to start on Sunday?

"11:00."

OK, I'll expect to see you getting started at 11:00 in the MORNING, and while you're doing that for me, I'll go buy another vase. Thank you… The carpet looks good. I think you got all of the soda out. Good job! OK, now, are you ready to talk about this coach situation?

"YES!"

OK, can you please promise me that we'll TALK, and that you won't yell or get upset to a point where we can't finish the conversation?

"OK, I won't get too upset. Now can we start?"

Absolutely! Just remember that if you get upset, we'll have to Freezeframe until you're ready to talk again, OK? Now, I have a question for you. What is it that you like about basketball?

"Playing."

OK, I understand. What else?

"Winning! OK, I do like winning, but being with the other girls."

Good! Now, what is it that you hope to get out of going to practice and tournaments?

"Being able to play."

RIGHT! OK, who is in charge of deciding when and how much you play?

"The *!&@%# COACH!"

OK, I do know how you feel about the coach, and I understand completely. But, let's look at this a little differently, and take your relationship with the coach out of the picture for a moment. Your goal is to play more, right?

"Yeah."

What would cause the coach to let you play more?

"If the coach LIKED me, I'd get to play as much as the other girls."

Well, why would the coach not like you as much as the others?

"They kiss up and are buddy-buddy. I don't know… maybe they just get along better than I do. I just say what I think. I don't hold back, and that's the way it is."

I understand. One of your best qualities is that you're REAL. You don't try to be someone that you're not. I appreciate that. And, I'm not suggesting that

you try to be fake, or "kiss up." If what you really want is to play more, then let's focus on that. So, even though you may not truly care if the coach LIKES you, you want to play more. What can you do in order to make the coach like you and let you play?

"I guess I can bite my tongue and not say anything. And, I can just not show it when I'm mad at the coach, because I see somebody do something stupid in a game, and they are making mistakes, and I'm still on the sideline."

OK. FANTASTIC! Those are some good things that you can NOT do. Now, what are some good things that you CAN do when you feel upset?

"I guess I can save it and tell YOU about it afterward, or I can just be nice, and hope that the coach puts me in... but I know THAT won't happen."

Don't give up just yet! One VERY IMPORTANT point that I hope you'll remember forever is that you can control yourself, but not someone else. So, you have to persuade the coach to put you in. And, if you can't accomplish that by doing all of the right things, like being at practice, cheering for your team while you're on the sideline, showing that you have a positive attitude, and just plain working hard to play your best, then we may have to talk to the coach's boss. And, if we see that the coach is still playing favorites, after we try all of the RIGHT ways to get you to play, then we'll talk to someone over the coach. We just need to be sure that if that needs to happen, the coach has absolutely nothing negative that can be said about you, which might be used as a reason that you aren't playing. See what I mean?

Also, you can STILL enjoy playing with the girls and get a lot of experience at practice, right?

"Yeah... I guess so. So, you mean that I should do the best I can, regardless of the coach, try to have fun, and not give the coach a reason not to let me play? I guess I could even be nice to the coach."

66

EXACTLY! I think you've got it, now! I wish that it would be easy to just do this instantly, but it may take a while for you to remember to hold your tongue and not let your body language or facial expression give it away, when you're angry. So, can we try this for a few weeks, and see what happens? Then, if you've really been able to do this, and we don't see any increase in your playing time, we'll take things to the coach's boss. Sound fair?

"OK, that's fair."

GREAT! Now, give me a hug and let's make a plan for dinner.

Can you see how the teen was able to de-escalate and get the problem worked out?

Can you also see that the PARENT was in control of herself and eventually, in control of the situation?

Can you see how the parent, knowing what to say, was able to set expectations, and help her daughter to make detailed plans for correcting the issues with the carpet, vase, and coach?

Can you see how if you don't argue with someone else, their anger runs out of fuel?

TIP!

Try as hard as you can not to use confrontational words. I used the word "NEED" on purpose, in an example in Chapter 7, to show what I mean. Mom says "THANKS! Now, you **need** to give your best effort, OK?" This is a mild example, but "HAVE" is very directive and confrontational to a child or teen who is defiant. If you use "NEED" in place of "HAVE," there is a difference in how some kids will receive it.

NOTES:

A child NEEDS limits in order to feel safe and to be relaxed enough to learn and progress emotionally. If APPROPRIATE limits are established in an APPROPRIATE way from the time the child begins to crawl, then your job as a parent is much easier than it will be for parents who, for whatever reason, were not able to do this. Sometimes, interference from another parent who lacks parenting skills, a child living with another relative or in the care of non-relatives, or, lack of good parenting information can prevent a child from beginning life with the understanding that "limits are OK, and it's OK for my parent to set them for me." Be careful not to set limits that are not age-appropriate, or limits that are not enforceable. For instance, you can set a limit by refusing to have a conversation with a teen while he / she is using curse words, but you cannot set the limit "you cannot use curse words," because they can do it when they are away from you, and you will never know.

SAFETY is FIRST, when setting limits!

A child who is "spoiled," does not respect limits, and is given things, sometimes, before he / she even asks for them. So, if their needs are met without the child or teen having to DO anything... they never learn to solve their own problems, and are dependent on adults... no matter how old they get. See? Stunted emotional growth. A caretaker who feels, for whatever reason, that the child needs to be allowed to have everything that he / she wants (or ALMOST everything), is creating a monster. The child will only grow larger and stronger, but will have 2-year-old temper tantrums... when they are **15-years-old**, and don't get what they want.

The difference in an older child or adolescent is that the child can now hurt adults, be more destructive, and even feel comfortable enough in the community to run away. This scenario is common among parents who feel the need to have the child's constant approval. The relationship is more of a "friend-friend" situation, almost as if the child and adult are equals. The problem is that the child or teen is NOT equally as responsible, or equally as able to function in the world and to make adult decisions.

Setting limits with a child who is not used to having them set by an adult is a tough task, and you will work hard to correct the ideas that the child has about how things work. However, this HAS been done, and you CAN do it!

There is more than one kind of limit. First, there are physical boundaries, such as a crib, playpen, room, house, yard, neighborhood, etc. As a child shows more ability to function safely and responsibly with a boundary, then the boundary can expand. Then, there are other boundaries... such as allowing family members to have privacy when bathing, waiting for someone to accept a hug, rather than climbing on them while they're reading a newspaper, waiting for a parent to finish a task before they go outside and play with the child, etc.

INTRODUCE NEW LIMITS PROPERLY by sitting down with the child (remember, we need calm bodies, and some level of eye contact) and calmly letting them know what the new limit is... and why it's important to you and to them. Then, ask them to repeat it to you in their OWN WORDS, so that you know they actually understood the information.

For the purposes of this book... and building a positive, healthy relationship with your child, "DISCIPLINE" is actually "SELF-DISCIPLINE." What that means, is that you want to train, coach, teach, instruct, and encourage your child...not order, yell at, belittle, or establish reign over him / her. We will be learning how to use LOGICAL and NATURAL CONSEQUENCES to teach children how to make choices that are better for themselves. If THEY make good decisions on their own, then YOU don't have to work so hard at "making" them choose the right path. See... less work and less worry! And... MORE happiness!

Think of the movie "The Karate Kid." Ralph Macchio plays "Daniel LaRusso," a kid who is being trained in Karate by little, old, Mr. Miyagi... an Asian Martial Arts master, who has what we might think of as an unusual approach to teaching. If you haven't seen this movie, it's worth seeing, as an example of learning through a positive approach. Now, Mr. Miyagi is not Daniel's parent, and Daniel is a willing student. But he does get frustrated and confused when he's been waxing a car for hours and can't understand how that can POSSIBLY be teaching him Karate. Finally, Mr. Miyagi shows him that the very same motions that Daniel has been instructed to use in waxing the car, are used to block punches.

So...the idea is that when we TEACH children through their own experiences, they become SELF-DISCIPLINED, and we get 2 "gifts"...

1. We don't have to be the "big, mean, parent."

2. We don't have to worry about them as much, because they make better decisions by themselves... they are self-motivated kids, who make good choices, and perhaps ask our advice in tough situations. Does your child ask you for advice yet? If so, that's a GOOD SIGN that they trust you and respect your opinion.

So...the GOAL of "discipline" is to set appropriate limits when we HAVE to, and ONLY when we HAVE to. **Allowing a child to fail is giving them an opportunity to learn. But, we want to set them up to succeed!** Please remember to ask yourself, before setting a limit or expectation… "Is this limit or request my own personal preference, or is it really related to my child's well-being?" Setting a bedtime, a time to awaken, a dinner time, and an expectation for starting homework or having it finished before watching TV or playing are ALL necessary, healthy limits.

I'm sure you've heard the phrase "choose your battles." Well, I don't like that one very much, because what we're trying to do is ELIMINATE battles. So… let's focus on getting you and your child on the SAME side of a problem.

Expecting your child to wear clothes that you like is not an appropriate limit. Expecting your daughter not to wear a micro-mini skirt, fishnet stockings, and stiletto heels in the 8th grade **IS** an appropriate limit. So is expecting your son not to wear jeans that sag enough to show his underwear when you're going to church. There is a difference between personal taste in style and appearance and in dressing in a way that can lead to dangerous incidents or other problems.   Setting "personal choice limits," discourages individuality and has no logical basis. You will not be dressing your child when he / she becomes an adult, so he or she needs to learn what types of clothing get the responses from others that they want… or DON'T want. Remember, as a parent, you are giving your child a series of experiences to learn from, so that they will make good choices when they are adults. So… let them learn to do it on their own. If you're embarrassed to go in public with your child because he / she dresses differently than you do, then just know that your child may sometimes be embarrassed by how YOU look, also! If your child or teen dresses in a way that peers laugh at, they will change on their own. Let THEM "own" the anxiety, and remove yourself from that decision as much as possible.

Oh, and by the way… please don't be embarrassed if your child has a tantrum in a store or other public place. Let THEM be loud and look silly. You keep your cool, and don't own their behavior… let THEM own it. Think of yourself as their teacher, not their parent. Would a teacher feel responsible for a student's behavior? Would a teacher be so embarrassed when a child or teen acts out? Maybe a little, but not enough to cause them to give in to the student or to start making apologies to everyone who sees the episode.

The same thing goes with letting kids put peanut butter on their cereal or catsup on their broccoli… or whatever else they do that's simply personal taste. Another important thing is to let them decorate their bedroom as they wish. If you have children who share a bedroom, they can either do it together, or each can decorate one side. This is crucial in allowing a child to have his / her own space and in developing their individuality! No, you don't have to let your teenaged son put pornography on his walls, but if your kids want to post photos of their favorite stars, or their crushes, or cartoon characters… it's **THEIR** room. By the way, there are a few products out there that can stick posters to walls without damage.

While we're in your child's bedroom… How clean is it? How much time have you spent cleaning it yourself or trying to get them to clean it? What if I took you off the hook for this one? What if you stopped asking your child to clean his / her room?

 What if you even made a point to ask your child or teen…

"Is your room clean?"

And then said to him / her…

"Well…it's YOUR room. So, as long as it's not a problem for you and you can find everything in there… and your friends don't mind going in there with you… and you don't leave food in there that might attract rodents or insects… I guess I'll let that be YOUR thing."

Maybe it would stay messy… for a while. But if you are a person who keeps a neat, clean house, it will rub off on your child or teen. If you're a messy housekeeper, then you have to "clean up YOUR act," before you'll be able to influence your child or teen. I suggest that your child changes the sheets on his / her bed, and you can help with that (depending on their age). I also suggest that if they don't remember to take their dirty clothes to the hamper… he / she will run out of his / her favorite outfits, and will be wearing some old ones that are too small or out of style. That's a NATURAL consequence that will usually cause them to start putting dirty clothes in the hamper.

Kids will value the opinions of their peers more than the opinions of parents until you have developed a strong, trusting relationship with them. And… a little of this is just part of them discovering (for themselves) what's "cool" and what's "weird." Again, if they are made fun of by kids for wearing something different, then that issue will correct itself.

So… you know that if you try to force a child or teen to take a bath or shower, you may have a power struggle on your hands. If they go to school looking and smelling badly, the other kids will not want to be around them. Neither will YOU. So, try… "I love you and would like to give you a hug, but you smell terrible, and I will hug you after you take a bath." The school should not call Child Protective Services on you for allowing your child to go without a bath for a few days. If your child's teacher calls you, let him / her know what you're trying to accomplish. Hearing the same, negative responses from other adults and children will have dramatic effect! It's how kids learn what's OK, and what's not OK in the world. They test the value of what a parent tells them by finding out if other people feel the same way. If their peers, or other adults say the same things, then it builds more trust for the parent.

Allow them to learn from their mistakes while they are young, because they are still forming the person that they will become, and the consequences are usually less drastic. SAFETY is first, though! Never let a child come into physical danger, such as letting a 5 year-old walk into a street or climb a ladder. I shouldn't have to say that, but there it is...just in case someone has a difficult time deciding which lessons to let a child learn on their own.

On the other hand, here are a few examples of **LOGICAL and NATURAL CONSEQUENCES** from my own childhood and from the childhoods of children that I've parented...

EXAMPLES:

1. One summer, when I was about 5 years old, I wanted to go outside and play in the yard. I wanted to go barefoot, and my mother told me that I should probably wear shoes... but she didn't "MAKE" me. So... being wiser than she was (that's a joke), I went outside, only to return moments later with a cut on my foot. I can't remember what I stepped on, but it was painful, and bled quite a bit. Afterward, my mother never had to remind me to wear shoes outside. I either wore shoes on my own, or was more careful.

   A **NATURAL** consequence... better for me, easier for Mom!

2. One summer, when I was between 4th and 5th grades, both of my parents were at work and I had a babysitter. I liked her, thought that she was pretty, and wanted to impress her... in my own, 4th-5th grade way. There was a wasp nest on the end of our house. And I, being the "little man" that I was... thought that I should be a superhero and get rid of the "villains." So, again, being such a wise child (hard to believe that I was in a class for gifted kids), I got a broom and began to hit the wasp nest. Well, I'm not sure that I impressed my babysitter, but I'm sure that I got her attention. I was stung several times. One of my hands looked like

the hand from the Hamburger Helper commercials. And, because I was stung at least once in the forehead. My eyes were swollen shut for 2 days.

This was a **NATURAL** consequence that I've never forgotten, and an act that I've never repeated. My Dad calls this "learning the hard way."

3. More than once, my father had asked me not to play in his tool box, or take his tools out of the garage without his supervision. Well, being such the "wise" child again, I wanted to build something from some boards that were in the back yard. Wouldn't you know that I got bored with it, left his hammer outside, and it rusted in the rain. So, instead of grounding me, or using his belt… Dad told me that I needed to replace the hammer with my allowance. Well, my allowance was either 25 or 50 cents each week at the time, so it took a while. But… it taught me that when I damage something that belongs to someone else, taking responsibility for it means replacing or repairing it… much like when an adult has a fender bender.

   This was a **LOGICAL** consequence… something that my Dad had to implement, but closely related to the poor choice that I made, and based on me taking responsibility for what I did wrong and making it right, rather than on punishing me or making me feel badly about it. I think that I asked for a raise in my allowance after that one… just in case I made another mistake!

4. I remember my father working in his home office, when I was… maybe 4-years-old. I disturbed him to ask him to tie my shoes. My parents had worked with me on learning to tie my shoes, but I had never tied it by myself. He refused to help me tie them, telling ME to do it. I couldn't believe it! Tie them, myself? I went into the living room, confused about why and HOW I was going to do it. My choices were to take the shoes off, trip over the laces, or give it a try. And, much to my surprise, I DID IT! My **NATURAL** consequence for taking a baby step was that I felt victorious, impressed my parents, and didn't trip on my laces. Kids will take a few baby steps and then have a failure. What we're looking for is more

baby steps than failures… not perfection. If you're a perfectionist, keep this in mind.

Tying my shoes by myself gave me a **POSITIVE, NATURAL** consequence. Because I was able to make that progress, I was LITERALLY able to "take a baby step" and not trip over my shoe laces. Consequences are either POSITIVE or NEGATIVE… based on our choices.

So, hopefully, you can see that **NATURAL CONSEQUENCES** occur on their own, without a parent implementing them. They teach people things from the experiences that they have… without anyone else having to make them happen. And, **LOGICAL CONSEQUENCES** are implemented by parents or other caretakers, but they are not punishment. They are a way of **teaching** by causing the child to take responsibility for "righting the wrong." They are DIRECTLY related to the mistake. You will sometimes find it necessary to resolve problems when YOU make a mistake. Use the same steps. There is no better way to gain trust with your child, than to admit your own mistakes and to resolve the problem. That sets a good example!

LOGICAL CONSEQUENCES SHOULD BE:

1. Directly related to the inappropriate behavior

2. Implemented within 24 hours of the inappropriate behavior

3. Done as a "teacher," and not as a "punisher"

A NOTE ON INDEPENDENCE:

When your child or teen wants you to help them with something that they should be learning to do on their own, such as tying their shoes, cleaning their room, homework that they are easily capable of, researching information on car prices, values, and repair records (for a teen), HELP them by TEACHING them to HELP THEMSELVES! Use these opportunities as positive, relationship-building time, but don't do all of the work. Allow your child or teen to do the work with your guidance and supervision. They won't learn if you do the work, because we learn from doing things, ourselves. "HELPING" your child means "helping them to become independent." THEY will feel more capable and YOU will have more confidence in them. Kids need challenges to become resilient. These challenges should be things that they are capable of, but have to work toward. Tell them that they CAN do it! Encourage them! **IN**crease their self esteem, **DE**crease your stress!

NOTES:

CHAPTER 7

Resolving Conflicts and Problems Effectively

YES! You've made it to the chapter on how to actually resolve a problem! I know that we've covered a lot of information, but the good news is that you have it to go over again, and again!

What does it MEAN to resolve a problem EFFECTIVELY? Well, many parents might say that if the problem is dealt with in such a way that they can go back to whatever they were doing before it began, the problem was resolved effectively. Some parents might say that if the child or teen stops doing whatever they were doing that was inappropriate, the problem was resolved effectively. I believe that for a problem to be resolved effectively, everyone involved needs to feel better about each other after it's over (even if they didn't get "their way"). And also that the child or teen learned and demonstrated a new behavior or new words that they can use whenever they have the same feelings or want the same things to happen. You WILL see similar behaviors and similar problems recur. Children and teens (and adults) learn by PRACTICING.

We learn best by repetition and by doing. We learn to resolve problems with each other just as we learn to solve jigsaw puzzles, put together Leggos, hit a baseball, throw a football, hit a tennis ball, braid hair, swim, play an instrument or work on a car. We learn by practicing. So, if you respond to a behavior with the same expectations, with the same phrases, and with the same demeanor each time it occurs, then your child or teen will become familiar with the steps to working through problems and will become comfortable with them.

Separate the CHILD from the BEHAVIOR.

Love is unconditional… not based on how your child behaves. But… LIKING someone IS based on how they treat us. It's a FANTASTIC idea to say to your child…

"I love YOU, but I DON'T LIKE it when you throw things."

"I love you, but I don't want to be around you when you whine. I would like your behavior better if you talked in a 10 year-old voice."
(Insert the age of your child there.)

"I really wanted to take you to the park today, so that we could have some fun. But, since you just threw a shoe at me and yelled at me, I'm not feeling like doing anything with you right now. Maybe, once we get this problem worked out, I'll feel better about you, and we'll try to go to the park tomorrow."

If it helps you to **separate your child from his / her behavior** to picture them as the cute, sweet baby that they once were, then use that to help. I know that when a child is making mean faces, throwing things, yelling, and having a tantrum… it's not easy to think of how lovable they are! Just remember that behind the behavior is a GREAT kid!

The steps are relatively simple, but the amount of time that resolving a problem takes will depend on your child's reactions, behaviors (or hopefully, WORDS), and on how you relate to your child. Resolving problems will become easier, and the frequency and severity of problems will lessen, as you begin to use these steps consistently. You AND your child are on a learning curve, and are experiencing a new way of relating, which will be strange and somewhat uncomfortable at first. Kids who don't have a high level of trust will not welcome change... especially if it means that they have to learn something new.

Remember the baby who had to learn to speak when Mom and Dad were slow in guessing why she was crying? Well, learning is WORK... and we learn when whatever we were using before to get our needs met isn't working anymore. If it WAS, then we wouldn't need a new way of doing things. When you are stopping their old behaviors from working, they aren't getting what they want. What they don't know yet, is that what they REALLY "WANT," is to feel safe and to have a better relationship with you. What they "WANT," is to grow up to be a happy, emotionally healthy, independent, productive adult. And, they can't do that using the behaviors that worked for them when they were 3 years old. What they "WANT," is freedom to do what they want, have what they want, and go where they want. However, what they want to do, the things that they want, and the places they want to go need to be appropriate. **So... they CAN have what they "WANT," if their "WANTS" are appropriate.**

OK, now grab some coffee or tea and get ready, because the next page begins the actual steps that you need to know in order to make progress with your child or teen. These are ULTRA-IMPORTANT! Within a few weeks, or for most of you, a few DAYS, you and your child or teen should know these steps and begin to become familiar with them. They will become part of your family conversation. Kids like things that they are familiar with... like camp songs, school cheers, or cool handshakes. These steps will become familiar, too... and soon, your kids will be able to lead YOU through the steps. It's even BETTER, when your child or teen reaches this point, because you know that they are learning, and that they have accepted the steps as part of their relationship with you.

OK, HERE WE GO! Grab more coffee, tea, or whatever your pleasure, and get ready to take some notes. Think of a specific incident that has happened with your child or teen, and apply these steps…

4 STEPS to Resolving a Problem

1. FREEZEFRAME!

2. CONNECT!

3. RolePlay, RolePlay, RolePlay!

4. GOOD TIME!

(These will be on the test!)

STEP 1: FREEZEFRAME!

Once you recognize that there is a problem (your child is having a tantrum, refusing to follow through with a request, not getting up in the morning, etc.), keep a positive attitude and HOPE that this will be a small one!

If it's something simple, like your child using a whiny voice to talk with you, or using the voice of a 2 year-old, when your child is 11…then just let them know that you need to hear their 11 year-old voice and that you'll be glad to talk with them when they can "find it."

If it's something more serious, then we'll have to "FREEZEFRAME" everything that's going on, in order to address the problem. Ignoring it because you're busy or want to avoid it will only delay your child's progress and reinforce the idea that you give in to immature behavior.

So, calmly let your child know that we need to resolve a problem, and you can even make "FREEZEFRAME" part of your household vocabulary. That way, when someone says it, your child understands what needs to happen next.

Stay in the room with your child, and ask them to sit with you. They can be anywhere within 3 -10 feet, or so… close enough to have a conversation, but in their own space. This is when we're looking for a relaxed body (octopus arms and legs), eye contact on some level, and for you to know that they are focused on the conversation by seeing that they are not fidgeting with or playing with anything, and by having them repeat things that you discuss in their OWN WORDS.

If your child leaves the room, plays with the dog or a toy while they talk, or gives you short, rushed answers and doesn't seem like they are genuinely participating, then let them know that you see right through it and you'll wait until they are serious. These are secondary issues that we have to eliminate, before we can really resolve the problem. For instance, if your child keeps getting up and going to another room, tell them that you will wait until they are ready to work the problem out. They are probably trying to lure you into a chase or power struggle… or avoid working the problem out. You're too smart to be fooled by that!

So, you go about your business in the house, and let your child know every 2-5 minutes that they can tell you, calmly, when they are ready to sit and talk. Remind them that they are on "FREEZEFRAME," and everything stops until you resolve the problem. What this means Moms and Dads, is that you don't get dinner for them. You don't let them sleep. You don't give them permission to do **ANYTHING** until they cooperate. This way, THEY have control over how fast it's resolved, and YOU don't have to be the "Big, Mean, Control Freak Parent" whom they hate. You get to be the "Calm, Cool, In-Control of Myself Parent" who can't be rattled by a child's behaviors and who won't give in to manipulation or intimidation, because you're SMARTER than that! If they **TRULY ARE** thirsty or need to use the restroom, you'll be surprised at how fast they can work with you to resolve a problem, so that they can get a drink or get to the restroom! Now, they may go to the restroom on their own, or get some water. If they do, remember that you don't want to stop them, physically. Soon enough, there will be an opportunity where they need your help or cooperation for something. You refuse to help them with anything or talk about their weekend plans, or whatever else they want to talk about until they work the problem out with you.

So… you go about your business, while checking on your child every few minutes to ask if he / she is ready to resolve the problem. But, if he / she begins to play a video game or watch TV, etc., you must intervene. Here's how you do that…

The goal is not to get into a physical struggle in order to "make" your child stay in a room and resolve the problem. They need to make the choice on their own. However, if they are being entertained by a video game, book, TV show, or if they go to sleep, they aren't working the problem out. So, we get in their personal space. We don't fight over remote controls or unplug computers. That only causes a power struggle. But, we basically "annoy" a child into working with us, because they eventually realize that we aren't going to give up or go away until they comply. This means that we are constantly interrupting them by talking to them… breaking their concentration on whatever it is that they're doing. We say things like "We really need to get this problem out of the way before we can do anything else." "I would love for you to be able to play your game, but we have to work this out first."

Also, it's important to be lighthearted and even SILLY when you're interrupting their activity. You can make faces at them, tell them jokes, etc. Just don't make fun of them by calling them a "baby," etc. Kindly touching their back or hugging them is OK, but if they push you away, don't touch them, for now. Just stay very close and very "present." Laughter and silliness shows them that you are relaxed, safe to be around, and that you aren't frustrated and worn down… so you're not even close to giving in and letting this go away!

KEEP THE FOCUS ON THE PROBLEM. Children will often try to change the subject… maybe even to something that you want to talk with them about. Let them know that you will be glad to talk about that subject AFTER the problem is resolved. That's leverage that you have. When they want something from you, such as to talk about weekend plans, to have dinner, or to be driven somewhere, they are more likely to get the problem resolved quickly. This step is the most difficult, because you are "emotionally wearing your child down" and proving to them that you are in this for the long haul. You're showing that you LOVE them, and that you won't give up on them, no matter how long it takes!

Once you prove to them that you won't allow your buttons to be pushed, you see through manipulation, intimidation, and other behaviors that should belong to younger children, and that you will see a problem all of the way through to resolution, this step gets shorter and easier. Your child will become more cooperative, because you are more calm, nurturing, persistent, and predictable.

Do you get the idea? If not, email me at support@honestparenting.com and I'll use your example to clarify this step.

STEP 2: CONNECT!

This is the "teachable moment" that you've been looking for. Once everyone is calm and ready to talk, we can actually make some progress!

First, we do a check with your child or teen. Do you have "octopus arms and legs"? Are you looking at me? Is your voice nice and calm? This teaches your child or teen what you're looking for, and they will soon gather that if they use a frustrated "Uh…YEAH!" then you will be waiting for them to relax a little more, so that they are truly ready. Continuing with a child who has an inappropriate tone of voice or who is playing with a toy or pillow will not get you anywhere. You've come this far. So don't settle for anything less than their BEST EFFORT. Give them TONS of PRAISE every step of the way, and for everything that they do correctly! **PRAISE and COMPLIMENTS are FUEL for your relationship!**

In following examples of dialogue, MOM'S dialogue is in **BOLD**. The teen's words are in quotation marks.

OK…now that we're ready, ask the child or teen to tell you what he / she thinks caused them to become upset.

What did you want? What were you trying to get? What was it that upset you?

Now, ask them… **Did you actually GET what you wanted? Did what you were doing work for you? How much time have we spent working this problem out?**

(Child / teen uses an appropriate tone of voice to answer the questions)

AWESOME! I REALLY appreciate you talking to me calmly because we can really get somewhere this way!

Now, what ideas can you come up with for something different that you can try next time, that will work better and will keep us from having a night like this one?

Keep in mind that whatever your child "WANTED" may or may not have been possible. Sometimes, kids' behaviors escalate because they don't get something that they ask for fast enough. And, sometimes, it's because they ask for something and they are completely denied. So, in asking the next question, which is… What can you do differently next time, to get what you want more easily? We have to consider that the issue may have been caused by the child asking for something, being told "no," and THEN resorting to a tantrum… because using words didn't work for them, this time.

If they say…"I DID ask for it nicely, but I still didn't get it." Then, this is your chance to validate tell them about a time when YOU didn't get something that you really wanted. This will put both of you on the same side. Then, let's go to…

 OK, it looks like you really did start in a good way… by asking. And, how did you feel when you asked to go to the park and I said "no"?

87

"I was MAD!"

OK, so you were mad? I understand. What could you have done to let me know that you were mad besides breaking the bowl or throwing the book across the room? Could you have used words to let me know?

"I could have said 'I'm MAD!' and told you why."

YES! That would have been MUCH better! So, then, what could we have done to keep you from being upset?

"You could have taken me to the park."

Well, actually, I said "no" to that because I'm expecting an important package and I need to be here when it arrives. So, what could we do INSTEAD of going to the park?

"I guess I could play with my toys."

That would have been a MUCH better choice for you to have made! You know, I think Mom made a mistake this time, too.

"REALLY?"

Yes. I just told you "no," instead of letting you know that we couldn't go to the park right now, but that I think I can probably take you on Saturday. Would you have felt better if we made a plan to go on Saturday?

"Well, I guess."

Let's role play that one, so that next time, we'll BOTH know what to do differently.

STEP 3: ROLE PLAY!

All of these steps are important, but this one is the step that will eventually help your child to replace the poor choices and immature behaviors with better, more advanced ways of communicating and of dealing with life's challenges. So... get excited about it, because it's your FRIEND!

Role play is important because kids (and many adults) learn better from DOING and EXPERIENCING things than they do from just hearing them. For example, that's why there are school science projects. It also shows them what it's like to have a HAPPY, SUCCESSFUL experience with you.

What we're looking for is a sincere effort. You and your child may both feel a little uncomfortable doing this, because not everyone is an actor. In fact, it needs to be sincere... not dramatic. The goal is for you to act out the NEW, BETTER way that the conversation could have gone... so that you and your child or teen can use your new ideas the next time a similar situation arises.

So... if possible, go to the actual room or place where it started, and act out the more desirable scenario once, twice, 3 times. Repetition will make the GOOD choice their **first** response. However... it may take a LOT of repetition, so be patient. Have them act out a GOOD choice that they can make the next time a similar situation occurs. Yes, you have to do it with them! This is relationship-building time, and it also shows them that they CAN make good choices. Change it up a little, if you like. If your child or teen can think of more than one good choice to make the next time a similar situation arises, then GREAT! Practice both of them! Have FUN with each other! Humor is GREAT in this step.

Also, keep in mind that if it's 2:00 AM and everyone is tired and emotionally drained, your child's "BEST EFFORT" may be different than at 3:30 in the afternoon.

Like parents who handle their kids' behaviors with methods that don't work (until they get new information), kids need new information to know what will work for THEM. This is like learning to play a sport or instrument… practice leads to improvement. Role playing isn't an optional step. It's the key to your child or teen learning new behaviors and learning to use words to express their feelings. It is a step that teaches and bonds the people who are involved.

PLEASE don't skip this step or do it half-way! Give **your** BEST EFFORT, too!

STEP 4: GOOD TIME!

Call it "repairing the relationship," call it "damage control," call it "Thank goodness this is almost over!" Any way you look at it, this is the last step… and it's CRUCIAL to your child's progress and your future relief!

With this step, you spend positive time together, in order to let your child know that they did a good job, and so that you have relationship-building time to draw from, the next time there is a problem. It's important to spend at LEAST as much time doing positive things together as you spent resolving the problem. This isn't ALWAYS possible, but you need to make a serious effort to do it, because even though you're tired, THIS is what lasts in your child's mind and heart… the fact that you love them and that "everything's going to be OK."

If your child made a mess by throwing anything, etc…this is when he / she cleans it. It's important to say… "Let's take a look at this room. Hmmm… where did that pillow belong? Where was that book before it learned to fly?" While you're asking these questions, you are supervising your child cleaning a mess, and you might even help a little. You're wanting them to be successful at taking responsibility for their actions… not punishing them. So, if they spilled something, you may need to get the spray cleaner and some paper towels for them. And, if they are small children, you'll want to help, and to make sure that you wash their hands after using any household cleaners. Remember, we're not looking for perfection… just their BEST EFFORT. You can even time them and make it a challenge for them to see how fast they can clean the mess.

NOW… let your child choose an activity for you to enjoy together. It can be a movie, a game, reading to them… or vice versa, cooking dinner together… whatever works, and is feasible for the time of day that it is. The point is to enjoy each other's company and to repair your relationship. The actual activity is not as important as the fact that you're together. Interact. Watching TV together isn't usually the best choice.

Please keep in mind that these steps can be used, to some degree, anywhere in the community that your child or teen has a problem. If a problem occurs at a store, work it out there!

EXAMPLE:

Several years ago, a woman whom I was dating had a son who was taking a while getting ready for school. She had to be at a meeting right after dropping him off, and he was going to make her late. So… needless to say, she was very stressed. She yelled at him repeatedly… or at least "encouraged him in not such a nice tone of voice." Well, all that did was cause him to be mad at her and to feel **the stress that she gave him**… not the stress of being late for school.

So… they had an "episode" and went to school and work feeling badly. It affected their day, although her son would probably not admit that he thought much about it. He may not have even realized that it caused him not to try as hard in school that day, because kids sometimes don't have the insight to connect their mood or behavior to a certain event. His Mom addressed the situation with him that evening, and he agreed to try harder to be ready on time the next morning. Well, kids don't learn immediately, and he had no NEW PLAN to follow. So, the next day was basically the same. Mom was frustrated and son felt badly about himself.

THE ANSWER… I gave her a pep talk, and here's what mom did the next day…

The son was running behind again, and Mom anticipated it. So, she got up a few minutes early to get her own morning routine out of the way. This allowed her to be with her son AND… to help him to get ready and observe what was taking him so long every morning. They barely made it to school on time, but it gave them a POSITIVE experience in their relationship to draw from.

That evening they sat down to resolve the issue together. First, they discussed his bedtime being earlier, because he was usually difficult to awaken, even having his own alarm clock. He didn't WANT to go to bed earlier (and tried to argue the issue with statements like "Johnny's parents let him stay up until 10:00."), but Mom reminded him that what other families do is not necessarily what WE need to do to be successful, and continued to ask him questions…

MOM'S dialogue is in BOLD BLUE and her SON'S dialogue is in quotation marks.

What happens when you are late for school?

"I have to sign in at the office."

OK, what else happens?

"I have to walk into class when everyone else is already there."

How does that make you feel?

"Embarrassed."

Are there any other consequences?

"I get a tardy mark and if I get too many, I'll have to go to detention. I also have to scramble to get my books and pencil organized when I get to my desk."

So…is it safe to say that it causes you some problems to be late and that you'd like to be on time?

"Yes."

OK…how does you being late affect Mom?

"I make you late for work."

What do you think that means as far as my work goes?

"It makes you upset."

I'm not trying to make you feel bad, but can I tell you what happens if I'm late for work too many times?

"OK"

If I'm late too often, then I look to my boss like I don't care about my job and don't want to be there. So, I will probably be fired and we won't have any money to pay the rent or buy groceries, or school supplies, or clothes.

"But you can get another job."

Maybe, but it might be a job that doesn't pay as much, and it might take a while. It's not easy to find a job if you've been fired from one. Besides, I like my job, and I shouldn't have to be late. Can you see how this is OUR problem, not just yours or mine?

"Yes."

Well, that means we're on the same side, doesn't it?

"I guess so."

OK...what do we need to do to be on time from now on?

"Well, I need to be ready to leave on time."

OK, and what needs to happen for you to be ready on time? What can we change? What can we do differently?

"I need to get up earlier."

That sounds like a GREAT plan. But if you need to get up earlier, won't you be REALLY tired? You seem to take a long time to wake up, already.

"I guess I'm really sleepy in the mornings."

So...what do you think that you can do differently to wake up earlier without being so tired?

94

"Go to bed earlier?"

YES! That's a FANTASTIC idea! And...I know that's not what you really WANT to do, but it sounds like you're growing up and realizing that sometimes, we have to do things that we don't want to do in order to make our lives better and easier in the long run. I'm VERY proud of you for seeing that! So, when do you think you should probably go to bed?

"9:00?"

That sounds fine. And what time should you set your alarm clock for?

"6:00?"

That sounds WONDERFUL! We'll give that a try and if it looks like its working well, we can eventually get to the point where you can stay up a little later. We'll just adjust it as needed. OK?

"Yeah... OK."

OK, what else can we do to help you be ready for bed at 9:00 and to make the mornings easier for you... so that you don't have so much to do?

"I can start on my homework at 4:30 and take a break for dinner, so that it's finished earlier. And I can organize my books and lay out my clothes for the next day, so I don't have to worry about those in the mornings."

FANTASTIC! Now, there's just one more thing that we need to take care of and then we're finished!

"OK...what is it?"

Well, I know that there have been several days that I was late for work, by the time we got you to school. But, I'm not going to count every minute that I was late or every day that it happened. So, we'll just focus on yesterday. I was 30 minutes late for work because you had a rough time getting ready for school on time. Since I was working with you on getting ready, the time that I had set aside to finish a project that morning was taken away from me. Part of the way that we're going to treat each other from now on is that when we make choices that hurt each other in some way, we're going to make it up to them. That's how good relationships work.

"OK, I'm sorry, Mom."

Thank you. I really believe that you are. And it's **WONDERFUL** that you can say that to me. But what I need is for you to give me the 30 minutes back.

"How can I do that??"

Well, I was planning to rake the leaves and to vacuum the house this Saturday, so I need for you to choose something that you want to do for me, and help me for 30 minutes.

"Aw Mom!"

The idea is that I can use that 30 minutes to do a little work, or something else that I need to do.

"OK, I'll vacuum for you."

THANKS! Now, you need to give your best effort, OK?

"OK."

GREAT, now what would you like for dinner?

This is a series of LOGICAL consequences, implemented by the Mom, and so her son is having to take the TIME out of his day to talk through the problem and resolve it. It took up the same amount of time for Mom, also...but that's part of being a parent. Time repayment is for time lost during a problem, not for time taken to work it out.

KEY POINTS:

1. If you've never had a similar conversation with your child, don't worry...it will come.

2. PRAISE is VERY important. ALWAYS recognize a "baby step" or any amount of progress...no matter how small! You need to get your child familiar with praise and comfortable with receiving it from you.

3. FOLLOW THROUGH! On Saturday, her son had forgotten about the vacuuming, so she gently asked him..."Wasn't there something you were going to do for me today?" And...if you meet opposition, just remember that the repayment needs to happen before going anywhere, having dinner that evening, or going to bed, etc.

4. Paying back time is CRUCIAL in working problems out, because it is a logical consequence, and because it shows the child or teen that relationships are about give-and-take. It also teaches them about how their actions affect other people, and helps them to develop a conscience.

5. ALWAYS end a resolution session with you doing something POSITIVE together. It can be as simple as a hug, but SHOULD be something like having dinner, playing a board game, walking the dog around the block, etc.

This positive time will give you the experience that you need to draw from the next time there is a problem. It gets the child to a point where he / she WANTS to resolve problems with you.

 TIP!

If parenting was a game, THIS would be your "Secret Move." How do you get a child to cooperate all of the way through resolving a problem and not just go to bed, leave the room, or ignore you?

Your child NEEDS you. Children need parents to feed them, to take them places, to HELP them in many ways. You do absolutely NOTHING for them, until the problem is worked through. This way...THE CHILD HAS CONTROL OVER WHEN THEY GET YOUR HELP. You're not "starving them" by not preparing dinner for them...they can have dinner as soon as they work the problem out sincerely. You're not "KEEPING THEM from playing with friends." You'll drive them to their friend's house as soon as they resolve the problem sincerely. Again...THEY have control over how fast it happens.

This allows YOU to go on about your business in another room (even if you don't have anything to do) and check in with them every 2-5 minutes to ask "Are you feeling ready to resolve our problem yet?" Children who are impatient, easily frustrated, and who want instant gratification will WANT to work the problem out, so that they can get on with their activities!

CHAPTER 8
CONSISTENCY IS KING...AND QUEEN!
Getting Parents on the Same Page

Whether you're together, or not, if there is more than one parent, there is a need for unity in raising a child or teen. Unfortunately, there are many situations where the mother and father have different ideas about how to raise their children, and that can be very confusing to a child... causing the child to be anxious and causing their emotional development to be delayed, to some degree. Let's say that you have 2 bosses with equal titles and positions at your workplace, and they are telling you how to do your job, but giving you conflicting instructions. Which one do you follow? How do you comply with both of their requests, without making the other one angry? It's similar for kids with parents who don't share parenting ideas. Of course, there are different rules at school, church, camp, etc. Anyone has to learn to adapt to going by the rules of different environments. The same is true with "going to grandma's house." Grandma may have different rules than Mom. But in general, parents will do MUCH better with raising an emotionally developed and healthy kid when they BOTH use Honest Parenting. For single parents, you may find that some things are tough, but at least you won't have anyone undoing your work!

I've encountered a lot of parents who welcome and seek out help, change, and anything that will relieve their stress and move their child forward. If you're reading this, then that type of parent is probably YOU! Your child is lucky to have you, and the world is lucky to have a parent who is interested in helping someone in our next generation to be a good, responsible person! Sometimes, the other parent is also interested and invested in their child's future... and sometimes, they are stubborn, uninterested, and often, just as delayed in their emotional development as the child. This can be a man or woman. We can't FORCE the other parent to participate, and certainly not to be sincere and to give their BEST EFFORT. So… sometimes, not having their support and not having the unity in how the parents both relate to the child can hinder progress. However… it will NOT stop it, unless the other parent is abusive. ABUSE STOPS EMOTIONAL DEVELOPMENT.

So, single parents and parents with "physically or emotionally unavailable" partners, you CAN still help your child to make progress. Sometimes, when the other parent sees that YOUR relationship with your child is working and improving… they BECOME more interested. And, if they are detrimental to your goals, sometimes, you'll make more progress **without** their involvement.

To reduce confusion, when you are relating to your child based on the information that you've read here, and the other parent is still yelling, using punishment, etc., it's perfectly OK for you to address that with your child. Part of HONEST PARENTING is to lay it on the table. It's OK to let your child or teen know that you and the other parent are different people, and that you are only in control of YOUR relationship with your child or teen. Your child or teen doesn't need to have one parent "badmouthing" the other, which is so common among parents who aren't together. **YOU BE THE GOOD ONE! YOU SET THE GOOD EXAMPLE! YOU BE THE ONE WHO HAS A PARENT-CHILD RELATIONSHIP AND NOT A FRIEND-FRIEND RELATIONSHIP WITH YOUR CHILD OR TEEN!**

Sometimes, when a child is having emotional or behavioral difficulties, it can be a sign of a dysfunctional family… symptoms of a poor relationship between the parents. If this is the case, relationship counseling or family counseling might be in order. If your partner refuses to go to counseling AND refuses to read this material and to seriously try a new way of relating, then I hate to be the bearer of bad news, but they may not care about your relationship and about the future of your child, regardless of what they **say**. This level of selfishness in an adult is difficult to change… not impossible, but very difficult. So, you may need to think about seeking counseling on your own, and about your long-term plans.

However, sometimes, parents "see the light" when you ask them questions like…

Where do you think your relationship is with our child on a scale of 1-10?

When was the last time you and our child laughed and had fun together?

How many times a week do you get frustrated with him / her?

How many minutes or hours each week do you spend having to deal with his / her behavior?

Questions like these may get the other parent to realize that there IS a problem. Once it becomes a problem for THEM, they're more likely to want an answer.

CONSISTENCY WITHIN YOUR OWN RESPONSES...

Please remember that we hope for consistency in the ways that parents relate to their children. You need to be consistent from day-to-day in the things that you say and do, the steps in which you resolve a problem, and in your requests, expectations, etc. Parents who have mood swings, who deal with each problem differently, or who set up a logical consequence and don't follow through with it will not be able to build trust with a child. So, it's important that your child knows what to expect from you, concerning the way that you talk to them, how you resolve problems, and how you give them positive attention (such as a pat on the back, a hug, saying "thank you," "good job," etc.).

There are several, unhealthy types of relationships that some parents have with their children. These types of relationships hinder the emotional development of children and can cause emotional and behavioral issues...

1. THE MILITARY / POLICE OFFICER PARENTING STYLE

The title for this parenting style is not a slam on military or police. I'm glad that we have the armed forces, and I'm glad for the good, honest, polite police officers out there. What I'm getting at is that you don't want a parent to treat a child as Sergeant Carter treated Gomer Pyle and you don't want a parent treating a child as a Police Officer treats a robber. True... people with military and law enforcement backgrounds are often trained to be harsh disciplinarians, and some do have power and control issues. But, so do other people. Either way... this is not an effective approach to building a trusting relationship, where your child is able to talk to you and is relaxed, rather than anxious and fearful.

ANSWER: If you have a tendency to bark orders or to be intimidating... or if you are just a large person who sometimes LOOKS mean... take that into consideration and adjust your approach when talking with a child or adolescent. Consider that you're dealing with a learning, growing child, and try to develop patience and a calmer demeanor. Relax...often.

2. THE SOFTY PARENTING STYLE

This is the person who values the approval of their child or adolescent so much that they often give in to whatever their kid wants... whether it's really in the best interest of the child or teen, or not. This parent will have difficulty setting limits when the need arises, because they have established a pattern of allowing the child to do most anything that they want. In 2-parent households, this is the parent that the child will ask permission from… because the answer is more likely to be "yes." This style doesn't work, because kids can't do whatever they want to in school, or in the community. So… it sets a pattern of behavior that will cause the child to get into trouble. It's also sometimes referred to as "Mommy's Little Angel Syndrome" or "Daddy's Little Angel Syndrome." Also, grandparents tend to "cater" to a child's needs because the child is a "precious grandchild," and because grandparents often don't have the energy to set limits with them. Besides… grandparents are usually sweet, and sometimes like to spoil their grandchildren.

ANSWER: If this is you, GROW A BACKBONE! Seriously… loving your child and being a nice person are GREAT qualities. However, you need help in being able to set limits, or you will do harm to your child's ability to cope in the world. You aren't doing a child or teen any favors by spoiling him or her. Instead, you are robbing them of the opportunity to learn how to cope, and teaching the child or teen to expect that EVERYONE will give them whatever they want. They grow to believe that they are OWED money, jobs, a partner in a relationship who puts up with their poor behavior, and basically anything that they want… without having to work for it or wait for it. They become selfish and self-centered, not to mention that they won't have many friends or successful relationships. Then, because they have no patience and no coping skills, you parent them **forever**. Do yourself, your child, and the rest of us a favor, and show them that you love them with a healthy, positive, give-and-take relationship. Start TODAY! It will get easier as you do it consistently.

3. THE GOOD 'OL BOY PARENTING STYLE

This parenting style is often used by "old fashioned" people who are resistant to learning new ways of relating to their kids. They sometimes say things like "What was good enough for my parents and me is good enough for me and my kid." Their style often includes spanking or whipping, grounding, and other primitive, ineffective punishments that cause a child to submit out of fear and not to actually learn to make better choices. Unfortunately, many of these parents are stubborn... and they will raise stubborn kids who will clash with them, and who won't trust them to be in charge. When the kids grow up, they become bigger, stronger, and less afraid of the parent. Then, the relationship involves physical altercations and / or the kid moves out at an early age. The parent-child bond that was weak, becomes completely broken.

ANSWER: If this is you, please try to have an open mind, relax, and let logical and natural consequences of your child's behavior teach them, in place of the "iron hand." Your life will be much more peaceful!

4. THE "BEST FRIEND" PARENTING STYLE

This parenting style is often brought about in families with divorced or separated parents. The parents compete to be the child's favorite, and become more "friends" than parents. Parents whom the child doesn't live with are sometimes more likely to form this type of relationship. BUYING your child's love can also go along with this style. Often, parents will shower the child with gifts and money in an attempt to be the favorite and / or to make up for not being able to spend more time with them.

ANSWER: Let your child be able to respect you. Buying their love only works for a while, and it's completely superficial. Not only do the bribes get more expensive as they grow older, but it's a hollow relationship that they can see through. The parent with whom the child lives will have an increasingly tough time if the other parent has this style, because they are usually the one who has to set limits and be the PARENT, while the other parent is the "fun one." For parents who are not together, but who both have the child or teen with them often, try to get along! Share this book! Do what's right for your child. Put any negative feelings for each other aside.

5. THE SIBLING PARENTING STYLE

This parenting style is often adopted by parents who are young, or by single moms and dads. It's a situation where the child makes up for the lack of another parent and partner. The parent confides in the child about adult matters, gives the child power to give advice and have too much decision-making power in the household, and puts too much weight and responsibility on the child's shoulders. This is unhealthy because the child has knowledge and responsibility that a parent should not burden them with. Also, the child is forced to grow up too fast, and does not feel the security of knowing that their parent has their world under control. This is a selfish way of relating that meets the parent's needs, but not the child's needs. And... the child does not usually become aware of it until they are older. Also, when this kind of relationship exists, and the parent needs to set limits or expectations, it is

MUCH more difficult! The child or teen has become used to being treated as an equal.

ANSWER: Find adult friends to confide in and to meet your needs. You don't have to be in a "relationship" or "replace the missing parent," just talk with other adults about adult issues and keep your relationship with your child a separate, parent-child relationship. Boundaries are there for a reason. If you have trouble with setting boundaries, then you might want to consider counseling to help you feel stronger in establishing them.

6. THE REGAL LEGAL PARENTING STYLE

If you are rigid with details or "legalistic," as in… making your child sign a contract when they ask you for a favor, or "mincing words" by holding them to 60 seconds, when they say that they'll "be there in a minute," this may be your style. This is a more intellectual version of the Military / Police Officer Parenting Style. There isn't so much yelling, but more holding the person to their exact words. This style is used by parents who pay too much attention to details… and maybe that's important in their work, but with relationships, it translates as controlling and mistrusting, and is counterproductive.

ANSWER: Well, Dr. Frankenstein, unless you want to create a monster, I suggest that you try to relax. Loosening up may help your relationship with your child or teen… and may help prevent a heart attack, also. Practice laughing! Practice seeing your child or teen as a living, breathing, dynamic, interesting, wonder of the world… rather than as a "project," or as someone who answers to you at work. Stop feeling as though you have to correct each little error, and choose the BIG PICTURE issues to deal with. Choose 1 or 2 goals for your child or teen, and work on those... eventually, with his or her cooperation. Focus on spending time together and building a RELATIONSHIP, rather than on the details. Really... once you do this, it's easy and fun... and you'll see cooperation MUCH faster. You remember FUN, don't you? It's what happens when you enjoy being with someone and no one is criticizing or saying anything negative, but you're smiling and making memories.

If you're an attorney, accountant, or anything else that requires precise information, and is serious work, then I understand the tendency to be legalistic. However, if you're in THAT much control, then you can also take control of your actions and turn legalistic behavior off, when you're around your family. Kids don't want to "walk on eggshells" around their parents. They need affection and approval in order to trust you to be in charge, and they need those things in order to be open with you and to feel comfortable talking with you about personal issues. You CAN do it! Oh... and if you don't, they'll become JUST as legalistic as you, and you'll have to deal with that forever! (OK... actually, only until the day you die... or, until the day that they are emancipated, or until you disown them.)

NOTE: Some parents may use a combination of these styles.

WOOHOO! YOU'RE ALMOST THERE!

Hi! Are you feeling good now? Well...I hope so! And, I'm proud of you for making it this far!

This chapter is about relationship building and Relationship REPAIR, as well as BEING a family. Hopefully, you've been able to have a lot of positive time along the way, but when kids have behavioral and emotional issues, it's difficult to find the time and energy for family activities. So, here are some suggestions...

109

1. One day a week (you choose the day), is designated "FAMILY FUN DAY." Each week, take turns, and let a different family member choose an activity. For the whole day, or 4 hours… or whatever is feasible for your family, everyone participates in this activity. Not everyone will enjoy the same activities, but the point is not the actual activity… it's JUST BEING TOGETHER!

2. Find a hobby that you and your child both enjoy. Even if you and your child don't already have a hobby, there are SOOOO many things that you could do together! Here are just a few…

Involving yourselves in Boy Scouts or Girl Scouts
Learning something together… take a class at your YMCA
Operation (It's a FUN, interactive game that almost anyone can play)
Volleyball (the whole family can play, and a set is cheap)
Exploring Woods or Hiking
Riding Bicycles
Have a sweet tooth? Try baking cookies together.
On occasion, almost EVERYONE likes to shop!
Nature lovers and artists might enjoy making Pottery and painting it
Drawing or Painting
A trip to the library or local science museum makes a GREAT afternoon!
Building Model Planes or Cars (be careful not to inhale the glue)
Gardening
Dolls and Dollhouses
If Volleyball isn't your thing, try Basketball, Ping Pong or Playing Catch
Collecting… Sportscards, Dolls, Coins, etc.
Riding Horses
Working on Cars (mostly for teens)
Chess
Martial Arts

Learn a Foreign Language
Sewing or Making Clothes
Using a Telescope or Microscope
Writing Stories
Walking
Fishing or Boating
Swimming

Also, watching a movie, using Play-Doh, or playing a board game are great ways to spend time together.

When you're ironing, cooking, working on your car, looking through your telescope, or doing other things around the house, try including your child or teen on some level. This will depend on their age, of course, but take advantage of the time that you have with them and multi-task. If you can spend positive time with them AND teach them how to do laundry, even better! You may, or may not, find them to be helpful, but you'll be working toward not having to do their laundry forever, and you'll help your relationship, too!

Make time to see friends.
Parents need a break, too!

A support system is important to have… whether it's made up of a spouse, family members, or friends who can take turns with you in watching the kids. We all have busy lives, and making time for ourselves seems difficult, sometimes. OK, maybe it seems difficult almost every day!

A balance between work and family is crucial. Kids who don't see their parents tend to detach from them. It's difficult for a child to

understand that paying the bills and building careers are important things. From their eyes, it can look like a parent doesn't care… and they will not get the help and information that they need unless you're there to give it to them.

TIP!

CATCH THEM DOING SOMETHING <u>RIGHT</u>!

Actually, "catching them doing something <u>RIGHT</u>" should be something that is included in EVERY chapter... because it needs to be in your life EVERY DAY! If the only thing that you can find to compliment your child on is BREATHING, then that's what you need to compliment them on! Sometimes, we need to start with "Thanks for brushing your teeth!" Or... "You did a GREAT job finishing your breakfast!" As time goes on, you will find more things to compliment, praise, and congratulate your child for. This will give them the self-esteem to make greater accomplishments. If they feel uncomfortable receiving compliments, don't worry... they'll be able to accept them, if you offer them consistently.

I WANT you to succeed in developing a positive relationship with your child! If I can be of further help, or if you need information on a specific issue, please let me know.

In Conclusion…

Hopefully, you've had a few "aha" moments or a light bulb has appeared above your head as you've read these pages. Hopefully, you are beginning to understand what Honest Parenting is about, and are excited about getting started! Honest Parenting is about several things…

- **Putting the safety of your child and family first**

- **Being a Good Role Model (because kids learn from <u>everything</u> that you do and say… not just the things that you WANT them to notice)**

- **Being HONEST in your relationship with them and in your responses to their behaviors and choices (this means no tricks, yelling, intimidation, manipulation, etc. in trying to get them to cooperate)**

- **Recognizing their behavior as a delay in their emotional development, so that you can see your child or teen as simply using behaviors of a much younger child, when they act out**

- **Being consistent in your effort… no parenting style will fully succeed and allow your child or teen to realize his or her potential unless you are consistent and use it daily, for months and years**

- **Dealing with any issues of your own that may affect your child**

I truly hope that you will take this information to heart and that you will ask questions when you have them. Your child is part of the future of the world, and you have a limited number of years in which to help them to become good, responsible, independent, successful adults. Use that time wisely, and you will be able to be proud of them, and not worry as much. AND… part of your reward will be that they will not be emotionally and financially dependent on you.

Any book is "just part of a deceased tree" when it's left on a shelf. I

challenge you to use this one in such a way that it becomes part of your family and of your daily life. Use it to gain knowledge, confidence, and peace in your home. OK, now go out there and make some PROGRESS with your child or teen! Then... tell me about it!

YOU <u>CAN</u> DO IT!

THE TIME IS <u>NOW</u>!

Before you go out there and "change your family tree" (as Dave Ramsey would say) ...

HERE is the GREATEST "HOT TIP" IN THIS BOOK...

 TIP!

PLEASE keep in mind that you can read this book OVER and OVER. Parents who have the greatest success in helping their child or teen to develop to a point where they are using behaviors and making choices that are appropriate for their ages do these things...

1. They re-read this information frequently, until they know it.

2. They LEARN the 4 steps to Resolving Problems BY HEART.

3. They TEACH the 4 steps to Resolving Problems to their whole family by USING these steps with their whole family whenever a conflict or problem occurs, and making it part of their household and family life.

4. They admit when THEY are wrong, so that they can use the 4 steps with their kids and show the kids that even ADULTS make mistakes.

5. They don't choose BATTLES, they choose GOALS… only 2 or 3 specific behaviors to work on, at a time, which their kids know about.

6. They subscribe to my email newsletter "A Cup of Honesty.

7. They email questions to me with specific details.

8. They use email Coaching and Phone Coaching when they become overwhelmed or need clarification.

9. Oh…and they refrain from smoking crack while parenting!

**CONGRATULATIONS!
YOU'VE READ THE BOOK!
Your "TEST" is how well you USE it!**

Always remember…

If you feel angry, frustrated, depressed, or have any negative feeling, put on some music, take a warm shower or bath, open the blinds or curtains, think of pleasant memories. When you begin to think positively… you will FEEL more POSITIVE! Teach your kids this, too!

POSITIVE PEOPLE PROGRESS AND PROSPER.
NEGATIVE PEOPLE NEVER DO.

We all live under the same sky and share the same planet… even though our "worlds' may seem different. Do the very best that you can with what resources that you have, and your child or teen should continue to grow emotionally. BE POSITIVE! BE GRATEFUL! THINK ONLY OF THINGS THAT YOU WANT TO HAVE HAPPEN, AND IMAGINE THEM… DAYDREAM ABOUT THEM… BELIEVE THAT THEY ARE PART OF YOUR WORLD!

You may email us to sign up for the email newsletter, to send a question for the newsletter, or to sign up for email or phone coaching at:
support@honestparenting.com

Made in the USA
Lexington, KY
18 June 2013